LAWYERING IN-HOUSE

I DID IT AND SO CAN YOU

STEVEN COVEY

CHAPTER 1

Introduction

In-house lawyering is different from any other kind of lawyering. It's different from working for the government. It's different from working in a law firm. A lot different.

In-house lawyers are people who do a lot of balancing.

They have to be part of a team and at the same time maintain their professional independence. Sometimes they have to know when being part of a team has become irrelevant and professional independence is everything.

In-house lawyers have to manage the balance between keeping up with the law and keeping up with the business that employs them. They don't get to just pick one.

In-house lawyers, working so closely to their clients in real time, need to balance speed and accuracy, recognizing that they need a great deal of both.

They have to choose the right balance between what they can do themselves and what they need outside counsel to do.

I worked as an in-house lawyer for over 35 years at International Harvester Company, which later changed its name to Navistar International Corporation. I was hired as a staff attorney. I was promoted to a managing attorney position. A few years later, I was elected the Company's Corporate Secretary. I got my first General Counsel assignment when I became General Counsel of the Company's finance subsidiary. And for the last 13 years of my in-house career, I was General Counsel for the entire corporation.

In-house lawyers develop expertise in the unique and sometimes esoteric areas of law that are peculiar to their company.

I learned a lot about Section 382 of the Internal Revenue Code because Navistar's net operating losses produced billions of dollars of loss carryforwards whose value (they reduce your taxes) had to be protected from things like changes in ownership.

When Navistar faced delisting by the New York Stock Exchange, I learned all there was to know about the delisting rules contained in the NYSE Listed Company Manual.

In-house lawyers' expertise is shaped in many ways by the circumstances of the corporations that employ them. Following are some of the ways my legal career was shaped by the corporation for which I practiced in-house.

Navistar International Corporation's origins go back to Cyrus McCormick and the invention of the reaper in the 19th Century, an often-told story that appears in most American history textbooks. The incorporation of International Harvester took place in the early 20th Century. As the Company grew, its portfolio of products expanded beyond farm equipment and included trucks, construction equipment and engines. The Company sold its construction equipment business in 1982. In 1985 the Company sold its farm equipment business and a year later took the name Navistar. Navistar continued on as a maker of trucks and diesel engines into the 21st Century.

The Company's business has been described as metal bending. We bent metal. And the metal we bent became farm tractors and combines; trucks and school buses; bulldozers and crawler-tractors; diesel engines and lawn mowers. In earlier years the Company made some of the first SUVs. They were called Scouts. Later came RVs. In World War II International Harvester made armored vehicles called half-tracks. In the 2000s the Company made military trucks called MRAPs (Mine Resistant

Armor Protected). And we bent metal into IH products that have all but faded from memory, like refrigerators and sewing machines.

I started working at International Harvester Company in the summer of 1981. The Company was, to say the least, in crisis. Within a month after my in-house career began, the Company executed the first of several layoffs that lasted through the end of the year. I thought I would be back in the job market any day. In the beginning I didn't care. Once I saw from the inside how crisis-laden the Company had become, I thought it was unlikely I would escape the next layoff, or the one after that. I remember saying to a friend of mine that "International Harvester is going to prove to be a decent addition to my resume on my way to getting a good job."

The Company's crisis was mostly about money. The problem was it didn't have a lot of it. What it did have was a lot of debt it couldn't afford to repay. Billions of dollars of debt. And it was coming due.

As a result, the fall of 1981 was all about debt restructuring negotiations. It dominated the lunchtime conversations of my in-house colleagues. I didn't know much about bankruptcy law in those days. But one of the lawyers in the Law Department did have some experience with it, and as he put it, "We're pretty much in a damned if you do, damned if you don't situation. Putting it another way, can the Company survive a Chapter 11 bankruptcy filing? Can the Company survive without a bankruptcy filing?"

The debt restructuring succeeded. Every single lender signed off. As one banker said, "If you borrow one dollar from a bank and can't repay it, you have a creditor. If you borrow a billion dollars from a bank and can't repay it, you have a partner."

By chance, I avoided my one and only opportunity to contribute to this historic event. On the day of the closing of the restructuring, someone discovered that a UCC-1 financing statement had not been filed. The filing office was in Springfield, Illinois. Someone came running to the Law Department to grab one of the in-house lawyers and send them to Springfield before the filing office closed later that afternoon. As it happened, I was not in the office. I was out to lunch. Literally. It's just as well. The attorney who made the trip went on one of the Company's planes and had a great time. He was the plane's only passenger. He was thrilled because the bar was fully stocked and the booze was free. I had to wait another nine years before I took my first ride on a corporate jet.

The bankruptcy that almost was, but wasn't, produced a darkly humorous footnote in the Law Department. In early 1982 the Company's Board of Directors elected a new General Counsel. The position had been vacant for over a year. The Board chose a senior partner from the Company's principal outside law firm. Right after the Board voted in our new boss, the most senior lawyer in the Law Department called all of the lawyers into a conference room. He told us about the new General Counsel. He said, "Now I don't want any of you to worry or to think that anything is going to change around here. The new General Counsel primarily is just going to advise the Board of Directors. I doubt that we will ever see much of him, if at all, in the Law Department."

He gave that speech about 11:00 in the morning. Early in the afternoon, he called us into the same conference room. This time he said, "Listen, the new General Counsel wants to meet with each of you individually tomorrow. He'll spend about 10 to 15 minutes per lawyer. And before tomorrow morning, he wants you to prepare a resume for him to review."

You learn a lot of lessons along the way in your career. The lesson I learned that day was to wait until you are sure of your facts and try not to over-promise.

In 1981, the Company sold a business called Solar Turbines. The sale brought in much needed proceeds of about a half billion dollars. Just after the sale closed, the senior Law Department attorney who worked on the deal said to me, "Now that we have that behind us, and with the cash we got from that deal, things should be getting back to normal around here."

A little over a year after the Solar Turbines sale, the Company sold its construction equipment business. That sale brought in less than the Solar Turbines sale, but it was still several hundred million dollars. When it was over, that same senior Law Department attorney said to me, "Now that we have that behind us, with the cash we got from it, things should be getting back to normal around here."

He was wrong both times.

Two years later the Company did the previously unthinkable. It got out of the farm equipment business, the Company's original business that had been founded by Cyrus McCormick in the middle of the 19th century. A year later, the Company adopted a new name, Navistar International Corporation.

The agriculture equipment division sale was announced in late 1984. Beginning with the sale's announcement, our Human Resources department began placing "dots" (figuratively, of course) on the foreheads of everyone in the Company to help sort out who was going where. Red dots were assigned to employees working exclusively in the agricultural equipment business. They would be terminated when the sale closed and then (probably) hired by the buyer. If they weren't hired by the buyer, they would just be terminated. Blue dots were people who worked either in the Truck Division or the Engine Division. Nothing would happen to the blue dots. It was good to be a blue dot.

Gray dots were the worst dots. These were the people who supported both the red dot businesses and the blue dot businesses. The Company would need some of them after the sale closed, but not all of them. Gray dots tended to be in staff positions. Everyone in the Law Department was a gray dot. Most of us, including me, spent the entire two months leading up to the closing wondering whether we would still have a job. The sale closed. The following day I got two new big assignments, the sale of a closed plant in Louisville, Kentucky, and the sale of a coal mine, also in Kentucky. My gray dot had turned blue.

After years of downsizing that witnessed the shrinking of the Company's workforce from over 100,000 at the start of the 1980s to fewer than 20,000 by the end of the decade, the Company began to grow in the 1990s.

The Company bought a one-third interest in a Conway, Arkansas school bus body company called AmTran. The deal created a memorable moment for me. We closed the deal in Little Rock, Arkansas on a cold day in December 1990. The closing was over by mid-morning. I was packing up and preparing to head for the airport when the president of AmTran said, "Say, if you have some time, let's walk over and see if the governor could visit with us a while." I thought to myself, "Just like that? Drop in on the governor? Without an appointment?"

But we went. There were about 15 of us, half from AmTran and half from Navistar. We were quickly shown into a conference room, filing past the Arkansas governor, who shook our hands and warmly welcomed us. I got ready for the inevitable photo-op that I was certain would quickly be followed by our departure. Instead, the governor invited us to sit down. And he talked with us for almost 40 minutes. He was personable and gracious.

The conversation topics ranged from Arkansas rice production to the Desert Shield conflict with Iraq. I confess thinking to myself that the governor of Arkansas must not have much to do if he could carve that much time out of his day to host a half dozen corporate managers from Chicago who didn't have an appointment. But after we all lined up and had our picture taken with the governor (at least I was right about that part), the other Navistar attorney who worked with me on the deal, said to me as we were leaving, "We just met a man who is running for president."

She was right. Two years later, Governor Bill Clinton became President Bill Clinton.

The rest of the 1990s saw more Company growth that came in the form of new joint ventures in the U.S. and new business ventures in Mexico and Brazil.

The big crisis of the 1980s had been about debt restructuring. The big crisis of the 1990s was about health care. In the early 1990s, a new accounting rule required companies to calculate the total present value of their post-retirement health care costs and show that dollar amount as a liability on their balance sheets. For Navistar, which had approximately three retirees for every active employee, the number was over $2.5 billion. Downsizing had produced a lot of problems for the Company but this arguably was the biggest one.

After lengthy negotiations with representatives of the Company's retirees, a deal was reached that involved changes to retiree health care benefits and the Company's contributions of stock and cash to trusts set up for retirees to help pay for their benefits. The agreement was approved by the Company's shareholders, who were told that the only alternative was bankruptcy.

Like most corporations, we worried about Y2K as the 1990s were coming to an end. As December 31, 1999 approached, lots of people got assignments. One of the people on my staff was assigned the task of putting a waterproof tarp over the top of every PC on every desk at our headquarters location. The thinking was that when the computer that controlled the sprinklers in the ceiling went crazy at midnight, and doused everything with water, the tarps would keep the PCs dry. Midnight came and went. The sprinklers didn't sprinkle. Nothing got wet. I don't know what happened to all those tarps.

In the 2000s, Navistar continued the creation of new joint ventures. Our JV partners included several U.S. corporations as well as companies in Brazil, India and China. We also expanded our product lines to include motor homes and military vehicles.

The biggest crisis of the 2000s started with accounting mistakes. In 2005 Navistar had to restate its financial statements, a first for the Company. That restatement was followed by another one that began a year later. The second one was a lot bigger than the first one. It required a long time to complete and produced a lot of consequences.

The Company had to refinance debt arrangements whose terms included immediate repayment obligations if our annual report wasn't filed on time.

The Board of Directors' Audit Committee brought in outside lawyers to conduct independent investigations of management to determine whether there was any wrongdoing. Those investigations continued for the next two years.

The U.S. Securities and Exchange Commission widened the scope of an existing investigation into our accounting practices. And then there were the shareholder securities fraud lawsuits and derivative shareholder lawsuits that arose out of the restatement.

Another consequence of the restatement was that the New York Stock Exchange delisted the Company. Stock exchanges have rules that say a company can't be on the exchange unless the company complies with SEC rules about keeping shareholders informed and up to date by filing quarterly and annual reports. And Navistar couldn't file any new reports until it had completed the work of restating its old ones.

When the restatement was finally completed, the NYSE welcomed Navistar back. They hosted a little party for us. There was a sheet cake. We held a Board of Directors meeting in one of the NYSE's large conference rooms. Next door to that big conference room was a somewhat smaller room where, several months earlier, the hearing was held that resulted in our delisting. It was more fun being in the big room.

We had our Board of Directors meeting in the early morning and then joined some NYSE officers on stage for the bell ringing ceremony that starts the trading day. I got to stand among the group of Navistar directors and executives as our CEO rang the bell. If you ever get a chance to do that, here is some important advice. Try to stand on the far left side of the balcony. The bell is loudest on the far right side. I stood on the far right side. It is a very loud bell when you stand that close to it.

Beginning in the summer of 2012, the Company began another period of downsizing that involved undoing much of the work we had done in the 2000s. We terminated joint ventures, closed facilities and sold assets. And one layoff was followed by another. And another.

In late 2012 one of the members of the Board of Directors talked with me about the Company's status. He said, "Steve, you've been at this Company longer than anyone on this Board. What's your take on what we're going through?"

I wanted to say something about the circle of life. But I wasn't sure he would get the "Lion King" reference.

I replied, "It's a feeling of déjà vu. In the 1980s, we dismantled a lot of things put in place by previous managements so that we could keep going. Now in the 2010s we're going to dismantle a lot of things put in place by previous managements so that we can keep going. For me, it means a lot of deal closings, and going to a lot of goodbye parties for departing employees, just like I did 30 years ago."

Five years and several rounds of layoffs later, that director and I both had our own goodbye parties.

And then the Company began to grow again. And kept on growing. The circle of life.

CHAPTER 2

Getting the Job – Do the Opposite of What I Did

If you are a fan of the 1990s sitcom, "Seinfeld", you may remember the episode where Jerry Seinfeld's friend, George Costanza, decides that every decision he's ever made has been wrong. He decides that he will begin doing the opposite of whatever he otherwise would have chosen to do. Within minutes, he has a gorgeous new girlfriend. By the end of the episode, he has his dream job, working for the New York Yankees.

My dream job was to work as an in-house lawyer. And if that has become your dream, you should take a page from the George Costanza playbook and do the exact opposite of everything I did. I will explain.

You probably are not like me. When you were in law school your career goal probably was not to get a job as an in-house lawyer.

You may have dreamed of being a courtroom lawyer, standing in front of a jury and delivering your closing argument, just like you had seen on TV. In-house lawyers don't spend a lot of time in courtrooms. We hire outside counsel to do that. Sometimes we go to court to watch them work. We call it supervising.

Maybe your dream was to work in a big law firm, rising to senior partner, where your compensation would be enormous and your contribution to the firm's success would be to act as what we refer to as a "rainmaker", the lawyer who brings new clients to the firm. The compensation of in-house lawyers is good, but it doesn't come close to the senior partner salaries at the biggest law firms. On the other hand, you never lack for rain when you are in-house.

Or maybe you dreamed of protecting society practicing criminal law as a prosecutor. Or protecting society practicing criminal law as a public defender. You don't handle much criminal law as an in-house lawyer. Unless you're unlucky and are practicing in-house at a house full of criminals.

I wanted to be a corporate lawyer, working in an in-house law department. I developed that goal through a variety of experiences. While I was in law school I worked full time. I worked as a teller manager for the savings and loan where I'd been a part-time teller during college. I liked that job. Later I worked as an Assistant to the Dean at a university, counseling undergraduate students who wanted to become elementary school teachers. I liked that job too.

Then, about six months before my law school graduation, I took a job as a "law clerk" (air quotes intended) at a mid-sized law firm in downtown Chicago. I hated that job.

It may have had something to do with the fact that I got fooled by the help wanted ad. The ad said the firm wanted to hire a law clerk. I thought I was going to be a real law clerk, doing legal research, writing memos, and whatever else real law clerks do. But instead, after I got hired, I learned that my particular "law clerk" job was to make coffee every morning, sort and deliver mail to the lawyers, do a lot of photocopying, pick up lunch for the lawyers, and act as a messenger, delivering letters by hand to other law firms in downtown Chicago. Sometimes I went to the post office to buy more stamps.

But what made my law firm clerk job even worse was the atmosphere in the law firm. At the savings and loan where I'd worked, everybody got along with each other. Same thing at the university. But at the law firm, everybody seemed to dislike everybody else. They were very good lawyers, as far as I could tell. Their clients seemed to like and respect them. But whether it was the pressure, or just bad chemistry, they seemed to dislike each other. The partners were mean to the associates. The partners and the associates were mean to the secretaries. And everybody was mean to the law clerks. In my case, it might have had something to do with the fact that I never seemed to get the lunch orders right. Whatever the reason, it was the unhappiest place I ever worked. I worried that all law firms might have the same unhappy environment.

After several months on the job, I decided that I definitely wanted to practice law in a corporation, not at a law firm. I said to myself that life was too short to be that unhappy. I stayed at that law firm for almost six months and then quit to study for the bar exam. Five years later the firm abruptly closed its doors. The legal press reported that it was a surprise move. It didn't surprise me.

With my goal firmly in mind, upon graduation from law school I sent my resume to every company in Chicago that had its own law department. And I got nowhere. I was invited to several interviews but never got close to an offer.

What I didn't know then was that most in-house departments made it a practice not to hire brand new law school graduates. Brand new law school graduates need additional training. In-house law departments don't usually have the time to train brand new lawyers. They need lawyers who can pretty much do the job beginning on day one without a lot of supervision. So instead of hiring lawyers right out of law school, in-house departments let the law firms train new lawyers, and wait for the associates to decide, after several years of working at a law firm, that their better destiny is in-house.

The first part of getting an in-house lawyer position is to not do what I did, that is, to try to get it too soon. There are exceptions. I went to law school with someone who joined an in-house law department right after graduation. She had a long and very successful career at her company. But she was an exception who I believe proved the rule.

With reluctance, I came to the conclusion that I would have to get some experience as a lawyer before achieving my goal of being an in-house lawyer. But I remained determined not to work at a law firm. What I did next was something else you shouldn't do. Several weeks after passing the bar exam, I "hung out a shingle" and opened a law office with another brand new lawyer from my law school class.

There may be worse ways to learn how to be a lawyer than to open your own law firm right after graduating from law school, but I can't think of one. Whenever I had to make an appearance in court, I had to visit the courtroom on my own time the day before, just to find out things like which side of the courtroom was where I was supposed to stand.

Later in my career, colleagues would sometimes say to me, "Wow, you opened your own firm right out of school? Did you feel like you were diving into the deep end of the pool?" To which I would reply, "Yes, it's just like that. Only drain all of the water from the pool first."

So far, you've learned that if you want to be an in-house lawyer, you shouldn't try to get the job until you have some experience, and you shouldn't get that experience by striking out on your own immediately after law school.

Actually, I was lucky. My partner and I practiced law with a degree of success for over three years. Financially, we broke even in our first year. We made some money in our second and third years.

But in our third year, Ronald Reagan was elected president. You wouldn't think that would have had much effect on our fledgling little law firm. But one of our specialties was writing affirmative action plans for savings and loan associations. It was a niche market but a good one for us.

A federal executive order, EO 11246, required every federal contractor, defined as a company that did business with the federal government, to take affirmative action to employ and advance in employment women and minority workers. And if the federal contractor had 50 or more employees, the affirmative action plan had to be in writing.

All savings and loans had federal insurance contracts for their depositors, issued by the Federal Savings and Loan Insurance Corporation, the S&L counterpart to the FDIC. As a result, all savings and loans, no matter how small, were "doing business" with the federal government. They were federal contractors. And as to the requirement for a written plan, a savings and loan could be pretty small and still have 50 employees, once you counted up the tellers, the loan officers, and the support staff. And at 50 employees, an S&L likely would have a personnel manager, but not someone who knew about the intricacies of writing an affirmative action plan that would satisfy an Office of Federal Contract Compliance Programs auditor. But my law partner and I knew all of that. We were in a good position. Until Ronald Reagan was elected.

Within weeks after the Reagan election, the U.S. Labor Department issued a preliminary proposal to raise the threshold for written affirmative action plans from 50 employees to 250 employees. That effectively ended our niche market. The smaller S&Ls would no longer have to produce a written affirmative action plan. And a savings and loan with 250 or more employees was big enough to have a specialist in the personnel department who could write the S&L's own affirmative action plan.

I sent out some more resumes, using essentially the same mailing list I'd used three years before. And about a month later I got a call for an interview at International Harvester Company.

I remember how eager I was for the interview. International Harvester was a well-known company headquartered in downtown Chicago on Michigan Avenue. The Company was then still in the Fortune 50. On the day of my interview, as I rode up in the elevator from the lobby to the 24th floor where the Law Department was located, I casually glanced at the sign posted next to the buttons for each floor. It was the weekly menu in the International Room, the name given to the Company's cafeteria. What caught my eye was that each day the menu included several flavors of Poppin' Fresh pies (the forerunner of Bakers Square) as one of the dessert selections. Poppin' Fresh pies every day? I wanted to get the job even more.

You would think that, even before learning about the Poppin' Fresh pies, I would have done a lot of preparation for the interview. And you would be wrong. In fact, I could not have been less prepared.

I would like to blame it on the fact that I was tired and still recovering from having just completed, and lost, a jury trial in federal court the day before. But that's likely just an excuse.

One of the first questions my soon-to-be boss asked me was, "Tell me what you know about International Harvester Company."

"Well, I know you make farm equipment. That's about it." *That's about it? Great start, Steve!*

My interview probably should have ended about then. Instead, patiently, my interviewer took the next several minutes to tell me about the rest of the Company's products, its global scale, and its history, including the fact that it had acquired other companies along the way, among them the Farmall Company in Rock Island, Illinois. I brightened and said, "Farmall? My father worked at Farmall! He worked there when we lived in Rock Island for 9 months when I was three years old. I didn't know that was owned by International Harvester. My dad always referred to it as just Farmall."

Now, I could have said nothing about Farmall. Or I could have said, "I know about the Farmall plant. My dad worked there." But no, I had to use the opportunity to provide even more evidence that I knew practically nothing about the company I so desperately wanted to join.

Then it got worse.

My interviewer asked me if I was familiar with ERISA. My mind went blank, sort of like the character, Ralphie, in the movie, "The Christmas Story", who sits on Santa's lap and, when asked what he wants for Christmas, can't remember how desperately he wants that Red Ryder BB gun. Rattled, I said no, the only thing I knew about ERISA involved some advice I had given to one of my clients who owned a small business and wanted to set up a pension plan that mostly would benefit only him but still qualify for the tax exemption. In retrospect, I can think of lots better answers I could have given. For example, only later did I remember that I'd taken an entire course on ERISA in law school. And that I got an A in the class.

And then, as if to remind me of how much I wanted the job, I said something about going to the Civic Center, the building in downtown Chicago that housed the Cook County Circuit Courts. The man I hoped would hire me leaned back in his chair and said, "Ah, the Civic Center. I'll bet I haven't been inside that building in over 20 years." I maintained my composure but what I really wanted to do was drop to my knees, switch into pleading mode, and beg him to hire me.

Here's why. I had been to the Civic Center so many times I'd lost count. And I hated the place. I always seemed to be doing something wrong when I was there. Not malpractice wrong, at least I don't think so, but wrong nevertheless. I would stand in line to file a new lawsuit and then learn when I got to the front of the line that I had to go the cashier first. Or I would take the summons and complaint to the sheriff's office and find out that I was missing some document that required me to retrace my steps and stand in another line. And in every courtroom there seemed to be some procedure, usually involving checking in with a bailiff or a clerk, that I skipped, only to be rebuked in an embarrassing way.

I would have given anything for a job that would mean I could avoid going to the Civic Center for the next 20 years.

The Civic Center moment should have been my wake-up call that I had to ace this interview from here on. And of course I didn't.

At some point I mentioned the fact that my wife worked at a publishing company about three blocks away at 180 North Michigan Avenue. The rest of the exchange went like this.

My future boss said, "That's interesting. Before we moved to 401 North Michigan in the mid-1960s, that building at 180 North Michigan was our Company's headquarters. So now there's a publishing company there. Does your wife like the job?"

"Yes. She was an English major in college, she likes to read, and so she likes working at a place where it's all about books. And she likes her co-workers. They're a nice group. Every Friday afternoon they all stop working about 4:30 and have cocktails. They even invite the employees' spouses."

"Have you ever gone?"

Now, here is what I should have said. "Yes, a couple of times." Or, "Yes, and she's right. They are a nice group." There must be a dozen safe answers I could have given.

But here is what I did say.

"Yes, I've gone a couple of times. But I don't usually arrive until well after 5:00 and I don't really like joining a party when I'm already two drinks behind."

I don't really like joining a party when I'm already two drinks behind! **When I'm already two drinks behind??**

Beyond the fact that the interview didn't end right there, here is what was so unusual. I have no idea why I said that. I had never thought that, not about that party, not about any party. That's not why I usually skipped the Friday afternoon cocktail party at my wife's company. And while I have never been a teetotaler, I am far from being a heavy drinker. One drink is my usual limit at a party. *Two drinks behind?* It may have been because by that time I was nervous, thinking that I had blown the interview. And my chance to enjoy those Poppin' Fresh pies in the Company cafeteria. And my chance to say goodbye to the Civic Center. So I tried for witty and urbane, almost always a mistake, especially at a job interview, and especially when you are not in fact either witty or urbane.

What might have saved me is the fact that, at International Harvester Company during that time period, it was not unusual for the Law Department attorneys to have a cocktail at lunch. Sometimes more than one. My soon-to-be boss may have decided that I would fit in perfectly with my new colleagues. In fact, I recall that the first time he and I and other Law Department lawyers went out for lunch after he hired me, he looked genuinely surprised when I ordered a Coke.

But here is what really saved me. Luck. Pure luck. Anyone who is successful and says that luck played no part in their success is lying. I was lucky.

My job interview at International Harvester Company took place several months after the end of a bitter and protracted strike by the UAW, the Company's largest labor union. The Company's current relationship with its unions was, to put it mildly, adversarial. It improved later. But on the day of my interview, the International Harvester Law Department had a backlog of union arbitration cases to handle. The Company needed someone who could do labor arbitrations. A lot of labor arbitrations. And my resume showed that I had some litigation experience, and, more specifically, that I had filed lawsuits, and even an unfair labor practice charge, against a union. And as it happened, the Law Department group that handled labor arbitrations for the Company was staffed by lawyers who all hated doing labor arbitrations.

One of the members of the Law Department, who became my best friend in the Company, told me about the staff meeting he attended when my new boss informed his staff that he was hiring a lawyer whose first assignments would be handling labor arbitrations. "Steve," he said to me later, "when we heard that, we all threw papers in the air and there were high fives all around the table in celebration of your hiring."

To recap. To become an in-house lawyer, don't do what I did. Don't apply for in-house jobs right out of law school. Don't hang out a shingle and try to teach yourself how to practice law. Learn all you can about the company before you go for the job interview. And don't say stupid things at the interview.

Or, you could do exactly what I did. And hope that you are as lucky as I was.

CHAPTER 3

Learn About the Company's Products

It was late on a Friday afternoon. The rest of the Law Department had already left for the weekend. I was still at my desk when the CEO came in and sat down. "Steve," he said, "Take a look at our new truck. Doesn't it look a lot better compared to the old one?"

He was holding up two 8 ½ x 11 pictures. Each was a picture of a bright red Class 8 International truck, the biggest trucks we made.

I looked from one picture to the other and back again.

They looked identical to me.

Not only could I not tell which was the new truck and which was the old truck, I couldn't identify a single difference between them.

Briefly, I thought the CEO might be joking. But I knew he wasn't. He had many excellent CEO qualities but a sense of humor wasn't one of them. I kept staring at the pictures, wondering what to say. Fortunately for me, he was so excited that he didn't seem to notice that I wasn't speaking. He began talking about the great new fairings, and the mirror placements, and the wider bumper.

Slowly I realized the new one was the one on the right.

I think the new one ended up selling better than the old one, so I guess he was right about it being better.

Learning what your company makes is important. Sooner or later, you probably will handle a matter that requires some knowledge of what your client does for a living.

I didn't think that way at first. I was a lawyer. I was expected to know the law. The law is the law. The facts are just what you apply the law to. That's why we call everything a widget in law school. When I joined International Harvester, the Company's principal products were farm tractors, combines, construction equipment, school buses and over-the-road trucks. I used to think of all of them as just widgets on wheels.

But a couple of early lessons changed my mind.

For one thing, I found out that many of the people who worked at the Company weren't like me. They really liked its products! They were just like that excited CEO. Whether they worked in engineering, product design, manufacturing, sales, marketing, distribution or even in staff departments, they were proud of the products. They liked to talk about them. If they got the chance, they liked to get behind the wheel and ride in them. They got enthusiastic when new models came out. It's hard to be an effective lawyer for people like that if you don't let at least a little of it rub off on you.

Another reason had to do with the background of many of my co-workers. Many had grown up in small midwestern towns. Some had grown up on farms. They not only liked the products, they liked the people who bought them. They liked farmers. They liked truck drivers. They cared about them.

Once I walked across the plaza to the front door of our headquarters building on a spring day in a downpour. I didn't have an umbrella with me and by the time I got on the elevator with my co-workers, I was very wet. As I stood in the elevator with rain dripping from my hair, one marketing manager turned to another and said, "Isn't this a great day?" The other replied, "Yeah, I hope it's raining all across northern Illinois. Perfect timing for a good soaking rain for the corn and soybeans."

It was hard to maintain my "widgets on wheels" attitude around people like that. Even for in-house lawyers, there's a lot to be said for client relations. Good to understand the product. Even better to understand the client.

But the main reason for knowing the products is what all experienced lawyers know. The more you know about almost anything connected to your representation, the easier it is to do the representing.

However, it's also true that you can go overboard on learning about your company's products. What you know today may change tomorrow. Product lines go through changes. Sometimes it's just the change from version 2.0 to version 2.1. Sometimes, it's new features. Sometimes a product is discontinued. Or something even bigger may happen.

International Harvester Company's Canton plant, located in Canton, Illinois, about 30 miles from Peoria, was one of the Company's agricultural equipment manufacturing plants.

I went there once. The plant's management had a dispute with one of its suppliers and needed help from the Company's lawyers. That meant me. I don't remember the nature of the dispute, except that it probably had something to do with the quality of the components the plant was receiving from a supplier.

To get ready for my visit, I did a lot of research on plow blades, one of Canton's products. The focus of the dispute was on two of the plow's components, the shin and the share. I had never heard of either. But through my research I learned that the share was the part of the moldboard that was positioned to make the initial cut into the ground and pull the plow blade downward to cut into the soil and allow it to be turned over. The shin was another blade that was attached in front of the share. The shin's job was to slice through the earth as the plow moved forward. The shin "delivered" the soil to the moldboard, which was at an angle that turned the earth over as the plowing continued. That's how a plow dug up furrows to prepare the soil for planting.

For a city kid who'd never been on a farm, I was pretty proud of myself. I certainly sounded like I knew what I was talking about when I met with the Canton managers. And of course it made it that much easier for me to talk with the supplier's representative to discuss the dispute. And as a bonus, when the Canton managers took me on a tour of the plant, I knew right away which were the shins and which were the shares!

I drove back to Chicago from my Canton meeting thinking to myself that I had learned something valuable and useful for future issues I might handle at the Canton plant.

I was wrong.

In less than two years International Harvester was completely out of the farm equipment business. The Company sold the entire agricultural equipment division and never made farm equipment again. The Canton, Illinois plant closed. Several years later it burned to the ground. Later the ground under the plant became just another environmental cleanup project.

I never had the need to know anything about a plow again. Just like that, my expertise in shins and shares became completely obsolete.

It made an impression on me. After that, while I paid attention to the Company's products, in the back of my mind I was always thinking that we were one divestiture away from my product knowledge becoming obsolete again. So I learned what I needed to know and left product expertise to the product experts.

On the other hand, if you ever have a legal problem involving shins or shares, and you don't know which is which, I'm the lawyer you should call.

CHAPTER 4

Rumors Are Just Rumors –
Until They Become Facts

In-house lawyers have one very important thing in common with their clients. Their work day is filled with rumors. What's the next big deal? Who's about to be promoted? Who's about to be fired? Is the Company's headquarters going to be relocated? Will there be a salary freeze? Hiring freeze? Of course, for every rumor that turns into a fact, there are dozens that don't. But that doesn't stop the rumor mill.

Right after I joined the Company in August 1981, the persistent rumor was that we were about to file for bankruptcy. In fact, I joined a pool with several other lawyers. It was a grim pool. You won the pool (which I think entitled you to a free lunch hosted by the losers) by guessing the date that was closest to the date when the Company would file its bankruptcy petition. The earliest guess was October 1, 1981. The latest guess was December 31, 1981. That was my guess.

Rumors being rumors, the Company never did file for bankruptcy. Nobody got a free lunch. Although it occurs to me that if the Company ever files a bankruptcy petition in the future, I would be the winner of the pool, since the date I chose, December 31, 1981, would be closer to the actual event than everyone else's choice. But it doesn't really matter because I can no longer remember who else was in the pool.

Everything seemed to begin with a rumor, including employee terminations. Working at International Harvester, and later, Navistar, meant getting through reductions in force. We called them "RIFs". They seemed to happen with surprising frequency. Over the 35 years of my time at the Company, I lost track of how many times I held my breath and wondered whether it was my turn to join the ranks of terminated Company employees.

I don't remember all of the RIFs, but I certainly remember one of the first ones, at least it was one of the first ones for me. I had been working for International Harvester for just under four months. For most of that time, the rumors about the next RIF were a daily topic of conversation.

The rumors became fact. It was about two weeks before the annual Christmas holiday shutdown, when the manufacturing plants would close, and we would all be on vacation for over a week. But there was one more thing to do before the holidays. That one more thing was a reduction in force.

On the morning of the RIF, my boss' secretary stopped by my desk. She said, "I just wanted to let you know that you're going to be terminated at the end of the day today." She said it very matter of factly, as if it were the most normal of occurrences. Maybe for her, after working for the Company for a decade, it had become normal. But I was stunned. She continued in the same matter of fact voice, "You are the newest lawyer to have joined the Law Department, so you are the one who will be terminated. They're going to try to get a couple of the retirement-eligible lawyers in the department to voluntarily retire, and that would save you. But I wouldn't count on it." And with that she walked away.

The end of the work day was hours away, but that day it took forever to arrive. I continued working, but I don't think I was particularly productive. Our normal quitting time was around 5:00. I figured they would summon me to my boss' office about 4:30. I sat and waited. 4:30

arrived. I kept waiting. Then it was 5:00. And I was still waiting. Then I started to get angry. Why did I have to stay late just to get fired?

Finally, sometime around 5:30 I got up from my desk and walked down the hall. My boss was gone. The lights in his office were off. His boss also was gone.

What had happened?

The next morning I arrived at work and learned that several people in the Law Department had indeed been terminated on the previous day. My boss' secretary had sounded so certain, that all I could think of was that they had run out of time to get to me. About that time, my boss' boss walked into my office. I took a deep breath, expecting him to tell me this was my last day at the Company.

He began, "You probably already know that we let some people go yesterday. Just in case you're wondering about it, I want you to know that it's over. There won't be any more terminations, at least not for the foreseeable future."

The secretary had gotten it wrong. This rumor hadn't turned into a fact. Or I'd somehow gotten a reprieve.

I told him how much I appreciated that he let me know.

Just before he turned to leave, he said, "You can be sure that as long as I'm here I will resist any move to get rid of you. You're doing a good job. And besides," he said with a mischievous grin, "somebody has to do the goddam work around here." And with that he left.

Ironically, five years later the rumor about his termination came true and he left the Company. The rumor about my departure came true 30 years after that.

CHAPTER 5

Take the Job Seriously –
But Don't Get Overwhelmed

It is a good thing to take the job of in-house lawyering seriously. It's serious work. Done right, it can accomplish a lot. Done wrong, it can produce disasters. In-house lawyers have a tremendous amount of responsibility. Sometimes the potential consequences of our work are huge. At International Harvester, and at Navistar, we seemed to have more than our fair share of existential crises that had to be handled in the Law Department.

Working on big matters can be simultaneously frightening and exhilarating. And sometimes, especially after I became General Counsel, it seemed like the Company's continued existence, including the jobs of everyone who worked there, depended solely on what I did next. Maybe that was true. But if it was, and if it has ever seemed to be true for you, I offer this caution. Most of the time it isn't. Most of the time, no matter how big you think the problem is that you are working on, there are bigger problems that easily put yours into a lesser category.

Not long after I became Navistar's Corporate Secretary, our new

General Counsel presented a report to the Board of Directors. His topic was the work of the Navistar Law Department.

He put a lot of work into the report. It was impressive. Slide after slide showed the magnitude of the matters he and his staff handled. The slides graphically portrayed millions of dollars in product liability lawsuits. The General Counsel presented totals on the potential dollar exposure of our many commercial lawsuits. He presented statistics on warranty claims. He talked extensively about the legal risks of our business and the critical need for accurate legal advice to the thousands of employees who made the Company's business decisions every day.

I sat in the boardroom as he made his report and thought to myself he was doing a great job of making the case for the Law Department as the most critical function of the Company.

And then, near the end of the General Counsel's report, one of the directors interrupted him to ask a question.

The director said, "So, tell me. What is the all-in cost of the Law Department as a percent of the Company's sales?"

The General Counsel thought for a moment, then answered, "It's just under 1%."

The director nodded and said, "Thanks. That sounds about right."

And with that, the director turned the page of his briefing book, a clear signal that he was ready to move on to the next topic. And in that moment, I realized that director was right. He had the proper perspective. I didn't. The Law Department may have been my whole mission. And it was the whole mission of my boss, the General Counsel. But it was just another piece of the corporate enterprise to directors who had to monitor and manage so many other critical pieces, like product development, capital investment, sales, engineering, distribution, and on and on. The Law Department was critical, but so was everything else. It was a great lesson in perspective.

For a time, I was the Company's principal real estate attorney. I was assigned that role after the untimely death of the Law Department's real estate attorney, who died suddenly of a heart attack after a long and successful career with the Company. My real estate experience in private practice had consisted of residential house closings and the conversion of an apartment building to condominiums. But that made me the most experienced real estate lawyer on the staff. It was an overwhelming feeling to pick up real estate files from my deceased colleague's desk and try to figure out what to do next.

Fortunately, many of the Company's real estate matters were pretty routine. Most of the properties in our real estate portfolio were distributor locations. Many of our dealers leased their dealership locations from us. The leases were not particularly complicated.

At the other end of the complexity spectrum was the fact that we owned the land on which our factories were located, acres and acres of it. And in the 1980s we shut down some of those factories. I assisted the real estate manager in selling them to third parties. It was easy, at least for me, to feel overwhelmed by being the real estate lawyer. Selling multi-acre industrial sites seemed to be filled with large and complicated issues, especially to someone like me, whose previous real estate challenges consisted primarily of arguments over whether toilet seats were fixtures or personal property.

One of my first "overwhelming" deals was to assist in the sale of the Company's truck assembly plant in Fort Wayne, Indiana. The Fort Wayne truck plant was an iconic Company location. Shutting it down and moving heavy truck assembly operations to the Company's medium truck assembly plant in Springfield, Ohio was a momentous decision. It followed that the project to sell the idled factories and the land on which they stood was a momentous project, at least that's the way I saw it.

One morning I was at the Fort Wayne plant for a meeting with potential buyers of some of the real estate. When the meeting ended, some of the managers and I walked through the assembly plant.

Truck assembly operations at the plant had long ago ended. The next step was to sell the small items of personal property. The Company was selling everything in the plant that wasn't permanently attached. We needed the money. Bins and crates were filled with all kinds of items. There were hand tools, coils of wire, spare parts, metal pipes and miscellaneous office equipment. The bins and crates each had a lot number on them and were arranged on either side of a very long aisle where people had once moved back and forth as they went about the business of making heavy trucks.

A long way down the aisle I could see what looked like a forklift with a man standing on it. He was the auctioneer. Today was auction day. The auctioneer was surrounded by a group of people who all had clipboards that described the contents of each lot. Some were farmers, many had come from the nearby Amish communities. The auctioneer talked into a microphone and took bids from the crowd, one lot after another.

I had never witnessed a live auction. It surprised me that it went so fast. The auctioneer would call out a lot number, take a few bids, declare a winner, and then continue moving his forklift down the aisle. His movable platform never really came to a complete stop. But he went slowly enough that the crowd could walk along with him, submitting bids and making their purchases as they went down the aisle.

The managers and I stood in that aisle and watched the forklift and the crowd of bidders move toward us. Finally they reached us. We stepped out of the aisle and stood between two of the large crates. Forklift, auctioneer and bidders swept past us, the auctioneer calling out lots and proclaiming winning bidders.

I turned to one of the managers and said, "Somehow I feel like *I've* just been sold." As soon as I said it, I realized I was taking all of this too seriously. I knew this was the first of many such deals I would work on. I looked down the aisle and saw the auctioneer continuing on with his work. And so I continued on with mine. Eventually I completed all of the sales, including the Fort Wayne heavy truck assembly plant, the facility that produced axles and truck transmissions, a parts distribution warehouse, and the plant where the Company's Scout brand trucks had been assembled.

Nevertheless, keeping a proper perspective was a lesson I had to learn over and over again. Around the time I worked on the Fort Wayne sale, I also got the assignment to sell a very large tract of land just outside Phoenix, Arizona. We called it the Phoenix Proving Grounds. The site included a very long test track, a large building where customers periodically were invited to product shows and demonstrations, and a substantial hill where various vehicles, including farm tractors, combines, construction equipment and trucks, could be tested on one of three steep roads.

The sale was going to be the biggest transaction I had worked on. I was intensely focused on making sure the deal was done correctly. It seemed to me that so much depended on my getting that sale closed. Feeling the enormity of the transaction, and with still precious little real estate experience, I took a trip to Phoenix to learn more about the property.

One of the local Company managers picked me up at the Phoenix airport and we drove to the Proving Grounds. There I met with the other managers. There were only a couple left, since operations basically had ceased.

Our meeting was in the building where customers once had come to see demonstrations of our vehicles. The managers showed me maps of the real estate and provided other details that would be needed for the sale process. They explained that the property currently did not have good access to water, a key factor in any sale to a developer. I took careful notes. Everything seemed to be a critical fact.

Then we got into a car and they took me for a drive around the test track. Next we drove up a long road to the top of a hill. The driver parked the car and we all got out. We walked around the top of the hill. The managers showed me the sloped roads that led down from the hill back to the flat desert. There were three, each with a different angle of incline. They had been used for tests of trucks, farm equipment and construction equipment to make sure the vehicles could navigate up and down steep hills.

I remember being impressed when I looked down the steepest of the roads. I couldn't have walked down that road. But the Proving Grounds manager assured me that some of our Company's vehicles could go up and down that steep road, and the tests proved it. I also remember asking myself why it was so critical for me to personally look at each of those steep roads. But I told myself it was a momentous project so every detail must be important.

It was a summer afternoon in Phoenix. The temperature was 115 degrees. I am not making that up. And it was sunny. I was dressed in a business suit, a light-weight summer suit, but a suit just the same. Here's why.

In the 1980s, the in-house lawyers at the Company followed an unwritten, but enforced, rule. The rule was that when we were anywhere but at our desks in the Law Department offices in Chicago, we wore our suit jackets. Our offices were on the 24th floor of World Headquarters at 401 North Michigan Avenue in Chicago. If we were going to a meeting with employees anywhere outside the Law Department, we put on our suit jackets and we didn't take them off until we returned to the Law Department.

The Phoenix Proving Grounds were definitely outside the Law Department.

I walked around that hill in 115 degree heat for a good five minutes or more, trying to absorb the significance of that hill to the sale process I was handling. I was wearing a suit jacket over a long sleeve shirt. My tie remained unloosened. I was hot, but I was determined to follow the Law Department rules. Finally, we got back into the car.

As I sat in the air-conditioned car with a question forming in my mind, one of the managers answered it without my having to ask. "If you're wondering why we showed you around the top of that hill, you should be wondering. We didn't think you really needed to see all of that. We just thought it would be fun to see how long it would take before you took off that suit coat. But we got hot and decided it wasn't worth the wait any longer."

I smiled. It was a very valuable lesson in maintaining perspective. The Proving Grounds managers had it. I didn't.

The postscript to my Phoenix Proving Grounds experience is that the sale did close. The sale price was well over $20 million, which indeed made it the biggest transaction I had worked on to date.

And as if to illustrate the point that no matter what you're working on, there's almost always at least one thing going on at the Company that is as big, if not bigger, than your thing, here is what happened at the closing. The buyer transferred the proceeds to our account. As soon as we received confirmation of the receipt of the money, instead of celebrating obtaining all that cash, we immediately wired the entire amount to a company that recently had won a multi-million dollar verdict against us for infringing one of their patents. We used the money from the Phoenix Proving Grounds sale to pay the judgment. So much for momentous.

There are many reasons why it is good for in-house attorneys to not let themselves get overwhelmed by the work. One reason is that when you take the work too seriously, the client's response to your work inevitably disappoints you.

After I had completed work on the third or fourth sale of an idle factory location, the real estate manager who had been my client left the Company and someone was promoted into the real estate manager role. One of his first assignments was to sell still another closed manufacturing site. I did the legal work for him. It was a lot of work. There were title issues, underground soil contamination issues, and easement issues, to name a few. But in the end, we had a successful closing. The closing took place at the manufacturing site, about a two-hour drive from our offices in Chicago. After the closing, the real estate manager and I got in the car and headed back to Chicago.

During the drive, the real estate manager reflected on the magnitude of the project and the effort it had taken to bring it to a successful conclusion. I knew what he was feeling. He was overwhelmed by what he had been asked to accomplish. It seemed to him that the Company's success or failure in the current quarter depended entirely on him. And in turn, that made him feel like our successful closing was a major event. He went on to tell me we had been very lucky to work on such a large, high profile project. He confidently predicted that our successful closing would earn us both big bonuses and promotions.

I felt sorry for him. This deal had been the biggest project of his career to date. And in his mind, that meant that it was as big a deal to the Company as it was to him. I didn't have the heart to tell him that today's closing was just one more in a long line of divestiture activities that had become so commonplace that they weren't big deals anymore.

In fact, among the projects I was currently working on, this particular closing would have ranked about third in size and criticality.

We didn't get a bonus. The real estate manager didn't get promoted. It ended up being one in a series of disappointments that eventually lead to his departure from the Company. He took the work too seriously, he let it overwhelm him, and he never understood why he was so unappreciated.

If your view of the importance of your work is not matched by the Company's view of the importance of your work, there is a great potential for disappointment. But beyond that, there is the risk that you can begin to take it all so seriously that you become a candidate for burnout. You can only be in crisis mode so long before the stress of constantly feeling that everything depends on you diminishes your effectiveness. If that happens, there are only two ways out. One: regain your perspective. Or two: leave the Company. I recommend the former. Because if you pick number two, the chances are good that you haven't solved your problem. You've just taken it somewhere else.

About two years after I joined International Harvester, all of the news seemed bad. Continuing operating losses had resulted in the Company's sale of its construction equipment business. Negotiations with our creditors were practically continuous as we restructured our unpaid loans again and again. Quarter after quarter, our financial results were disappointing. Cash flow was an issue, putting pressure on those of us working on even minor divestiture deals to conclude them quickly. I was feeling overwhelmed by the problems on my desk, which seemed to perfectly mirror the dire straits the Company found itself in. Worse, the problems had been plaguing me for a long time and there seemed to be no end in sight for any of them.

And then one evening on the commuter train, I read a magazine article about coping with stress. The author suggested that you make a list of the five biggest problems in your work, then put the list in an envelope and put the envelope in your desk, and then six months later pull it out to see if those problems were as big as you thought.

I had nothing to lose. I made a list. I put it in an envelope. I put the envelope in a desk drawer in my office. Ironically, I was so busy that I forgot about bringing the list out and reading it at the six-month mark. In fact, I completely forgot about it. It must not have been in a desk drawer that I opened very often, or maybe it was underneath other papers. But it wasn't until about a year after I'd written that list that I happened to see it again.

I opened it and read the five items it contained. Five gigantic problems, all of which had to be successfully handled, and all of which depended on me. And as I read through them, I got a huge shock.

Of the five items, three of them had successfully concluded and had not been nearly as harrowing in their resolution as I had imagined they might be. One of the five items was still around but it was satisfactorily progressing and was no longer a big problem. In fact, if I were to make a new top five list, this item wouldn't even be close to making the list.

And the fifth item? As I read it, I couldn't remember it. It must have gone away right after I wrote the list. Granted, it had been a year. But the fact that I could not remember it was startling to me.

You should always take the job seriously. But once in a while, write out that list. Whether you remember to check it six months later or six years later, I guarantee you it will be the perspective restorer you need.

CHAPTER 6

Tell the Story – Even If You Think You Don't Have To

In-house lawyering is a lot about storytelling. For that matter, lawyering of any kind is a lot about storytelling.

When I was still practicing on my own, before I became an in-house lawyer, I handled a divorce. My client was the wife of a husband who cheated on her with another woman. The husband and the other woman stole some money that belonged to my client and then left town together. My client hadn't heard from him since the day he left, more than three years before she retained me.

At that time in Illinois, divorce cases required a reason. You had to have "cause" for divorce. My client had adultery going for her. That was one of the acceptable causes. But adultery presented proof problems, since I had no idea how to find, and serve, the wandering husband and the woman with whom he'd cheated.

But when I looked at the divorce statute, I saw that "abandonment" was a valid cause. Abandonment was defined as one of the spouses leaving the other spouse and not coming home for at least two years. My client's husband had been gone a comfortable three years. Perfect.

If "easy peasy" had been a phrase in the 1970s, that's what I would have said to myself.

I prepared the divorce petition, seeking a dissolution of the marriage because of the husband's abandonment, and my client and I went to court.

I should have known. The box of tissues prominently displayed on the witness stand should have been the only clue I needed. But I was still pretty new at lawyering. Our case was called. I introduced myself to the judge. I put my client on the stand and had her recite that her husband had been gone for over three years and she hadn't heard from him. Done. I asked the judge to grant the divorce to my client on the grounds of abandonment.

The judge looked at me. "Counselor," he said. "It doesn't appear to me that you've established that the husband has truly abandoned this marriage. I mean, has she tried to find him? Does she know why he's been gone so long?"

My mind raced. Was that in the statute? She was supposed to look for him? Didn't it just say he had to be gone for a specified period of time? What should I say next?

But my client was smarter than I was. She turned to the judge, and in an emotional voice, she said, "Oh, judge, my husband is a bad man. He was sleeping with the woman next door. When I caught them, they ran away together. But first they stole money from me. I don't ever want to see him again."

The judge turned to me. "Counselor, did you know all this?"

"Yes, your honor," I said. "But my client preferred not to have to relive this sordid story, and so we have asked for this divorce based on the husband's abandonment of the marriage."

The judge scowled. He granted the divorce. But I had no doubts as to who had really gotten the job done. And it wasn't me. Afterward, as she thanked me for my work, my client said, "He was a nice man, the judge. He just wanted to hear the story."

I had forgotten that incident, and the lesson it taught me, by the time I had been at International Harvester Company for several years. I suppose I could make myself feel better by noting that my work in-house didn't require me to handle divorces. But the "tell the story" story offered a more universal lesson than that.

Sometime in the 1980s I handled the case of an International Harvester employee who had gotten fired. Everyone agreed she was a bad employee. Her file was filled with warnings and disciplinary actions. And so one day she was called into a conference room and informed that she was being terminated.

But this termination took place before Human Resources managers realized that employees should be accompanied by someone in management when they returned to their desks to gather personal items. It was one of the lessons they hadn't learned yet.

This particular terminated employee went back to her desk, packed up her things, and then proceeded to trash the computer she had been using. Lots of data was lost. And the computer was broken beyond repair. I forget the details of how she did it, but I remember she was thorough. I think a hammer might have been involved. Or maybe scissors. The damage she had done was considerable. Estimates were that a replacement computer would cost several thousand dollars. And considerable effort and expense would be required to restore the data she'd erased.

It was not a big surprise that Human Resources decided they would partially reimburse the Company for the damage by not paying the former employee the unused vacation pay that she otherwise would have received under our termination policies.

The former employee demanded the money. Management refused. The former employee filed a claim for unpaid wages with the state Labor Department. That's how I got involved. Someone had to go represent the Company at a hearing before the state Labor Department hearing officer.

It didn't require a lot of legal research to see that the employee had chosen the wrong place to seek her vacation pay. The only place her claim could be presented was in a federal court. I could win the case based on the doctrine of federal preemption, a fancy sounding phrase I had learned in law school. It was a technical out, but it was ironclad.

On the morning of the hearing, I was ready. I had my talking points all prepared. I would explain to the hearing officer that he had to dismiss the claim because it arose under ERISA and the doctrine of federal preemption precluded an exercise of jurisdiction by the state Labor Department.

And then the phone rang. It was one of the outside counsel with whom I regularly worked. He was calling about something else. I told him I had to hang up because I had to go present this federal preemption argument. I had a lot of respect for this particular lawyer, so when he asked me to tell him more about the case, I took the time to do it. I told him about the bad employee, how many times she'd been late, or not shown up at work at all. I told him about the poor quality of her work. And I told him about how she'd smashed one of our computers and erased data and how much it had cost us.

When I was finished, he said, "You should tell that story to the hearing officer."

I was surprised. I said, "Why? I don't need the story. I have this federal preemption thing. It's a sure winner."

He replied, "I'm sure your argument is solid, but the hearing officer is a person. And people want to feel good about the decisions they make. It will help the hearing officer feel better about accepting your legal argument if he hears the story and can see that she doesn't deserve the money."

I knew he was right. My divorce story from years before came back to me. Substitute "preemption" for "abandonment", and essentially it was the same story.

I went to the hearing. I told the entire story of the former employee to the hearing officer. When I was done with the story, I said, "And in addition to causing cost and unnecessary work for us at International Harvester Company, the former employee is now causing unnecessary work for you. Because the only place to bring this claim is in federal court, not here. The state Labor Department has no jurisdiction to deal with it. It's called the doctrine of federal preemption."

I won. The hearing officer agreed that his office had no jurisdiction. Maybe I would have won anyway. But I never forgot the lesson again. I settled into my role as storyteller.

Many years later, at my going away dinner, several of the guests spoke. They said nice things about me, the kind of things you would expect to hear at a retirement party at the conclusion of a long career.

Then it was my turn to speak.

I said, "I have been thinking about what the job of an in-house lawyer really requires. And when you come down to it, what you need most is to be a good storyteller. For over 35 years, I have had the privilege to tell your stories, and the stories of the men and women who worked at Navistar before you. I told your stories to judges and juries. I told your stories to regulators and prosecutors, to opposing lawyers and business partners. And I want to thank you for giving me stories I could be proud to tell. Stories of people who consistently worked hard, did the best they could, and did what they believed was right. No lawyer could have asked for more."

It was my last story at Navistar. It was a short story. It's my favorite story.

CHAPTER 7

Stay Where You Are

It's challenging to work in an in-house law department. In-house lawyers' fortunes tend to rise and fall with the fortunes of the company that employs them. You can win all your cases, close all your deals successfully and under budget, and collect all monies due your client, but if your client's business loses money, so do you. It doesn't matter that you had a stellar year. If sales are off, then bonuses are reduced or are non-existent. Salaries get frozen. The stock market passes its judgment, and you watch the value of your stock options go down.

And here's an odd irony that adds to the challenge. When your company is experiencing good times, you, the in-house lawyer, share in the increased compensation just like all of the other employees. But here is the irony. You tend to be less busy during those good times. The company's suppliers, dealers and employees tend to be happier and more satisfied when the company is prospering, and that usually means fewer lawsuits.

And the opposite also is true. In hard times, the in-house lawyers experience salary freezes and non-existent bonus pools, but nevertheless are busier. That's because in hard times the company turns to its lawyers to work on deals that will produce the synergies needed to offset sliding sales and market share. You work on buying competitors when their price is low. And along with those deals come divestiture deals to generate the cash your company needs to get through the latest downturn (and to finance the purchase of those competitors). And of course, the number of lawsuits filed against your company seems to go up during hard economic times. I used to think that some plaintiffs just liked kicking you when you were down. But that's probably not true. Probably.

That curious counter-cyclicality between the workload/rewards of the law department and the workload/rewards of the rest of the company could also make you think about leaving the law department, giving up in-house lawyering in favor of a job elsewhere in the company.

During my time at the Company I was offered two jobs outside the Law Department. I turned both of them down. The decision each time was difficult. Each time I was being offered a bigger title and a bigger salary. But I decided to stay where I was. I wouldn't go so far as to say you should make the same decisions I made if you get offered a job in another part of your company. I can only say that I am pretty sure my career would not have been as successful if I had left the Law Department.

And if all of those challenges and ironies aren't enough, you can throw in the paranoia surrounding the ever-present fear that your client's weakened condition during the down part of the business cycle will make it a takeover target. Maybe it's not the case at every public corporation, but at International Harvester Company, and later Navistar, there was almost always a rumor circulating about someone buying us. In no particular order, the rumored purchaser of our Company was Caterpillar; Deere; Chrysler; General Motors; Ford; Paccar; Volvo; Freightliner; Mack Trucks; Nissan; Fiat; Toyota; KKR; Hino; Mahindra & Mahindra; and Dina Camiones.

And those were just the rumors I heard about. None came true, mostly because their origin usually was nothing more than speculation. But each sent a shudder through our Law Department. I was in more than one conversation with my colleagues about what would happen to our Law Department once the new owner took over. Would we have to move to Detroit? Would they hire any of us or just use their own lawyers? Would we have to learn how to speak Japanese? And so on. In the 35 ½ years I worked at the Company, there never was a new owner, but that didn't stop the conversations.

If you are practicing law inside a corporation, and your client is in a cyclical business (and in the end, whose client isn't?), or going through a downsizing, or the subject of takeover rumors, it's natural for your thoughts to drift in the direction of leaving your current client and finding a more stable, prosperous one to work for. And if you definitely have made up your mind to find work in another corporate law department, the advice that follows is not for you. You should go.

But if there's any indecision left in your thought process, I will share with you why I stayed, and why, in the end, I was glad I did.

First, there is the problem of grass looking greener on the other side of the corporate fence. This may seem like an obvious reason to pause before switching clients, but it didn't always occur to the in-house lawyers with whom I worked.

More than one of my Law Department colleagues at Navistar left the Company to join in-house law departments at corporations that: promptly relocated (to places my colleagues didn't want to go); or got sold (to corporations that already had their own in-house law departments and didn't need more lawyers); or corporations that themselves fell on hard times. When it comes to corporate grass, green can turn to brown fast.

For example, right after I graduated from law school, I interviewed to be an in-house lawyer at Continental Illinois National Bank in Chicago. I wanted that job so much. I didn't get it. I've never known why. Maybe it's better not knowing. Anyway, five years later, right after I was hired at International Harvester Company, Continental Bank "experimented" with the idea of eliminating all of its in-house lawyers. Just like that, the bank's law department functions all were assumed by an outside law firm. Some years after that, Continental Illinois National Bank went the way of its law department and itself ceased to exist. I always liked to think it was because they'd gotten rid of their in-house lawyers. But I suspect it was a little more complicated than that.

About a year after I joined International Harvester Company, and about the time the Company was embarking on another round of divestitures and downsizing, I applied for an in-house lawyer job at Dart & Kraft. The grass looked a lot greener there. One member of the International Harvester Law Department had already gone there and was doing well. Dart & Kraft, the result of a merger several years before between Dart Industries and Kraft Foods, seemed to have a better future than "ailing and failing International Harvester", the media term often used to describe the Company.

At the time I thought the interviews at Dart & Kraft went well. In retrospect, it probably wasn't a good idea for me to say to the lawyers who interviewed me that, at International Harvester, the crises came to the Law Department with such regularity that I had had the equivalent of 10 years experience in one year of practice. It didn't occur to me until later that it probably wasn't a smart idea to tell in-house lawyers at another company that I had been through way more than they had. I must have come across as arrogant. But I was younger then. Anyway, I didn't get the job. I was disappointed, but I forgot about Dart & Kraft until several years later when they were acquired by Phillip Morris Companies. It made me wonder how I, a non-smoker, would have fared in the post-acquisition Dart & Kraft law department. I'm guessing not so well.

Of course there always are exceptions. One of my Law Department colleagues left International Harvester and became General Counsel of a sizable public company. I was particularly interested in his story because I was hired as his replacement at International Harvester's Law Department. Not long after my predecessor left International Harvester, he was elected CEO at his new company. So, for him, leaving the Company worked out. But on balance, I have to say that for every story with a happy ending like that one (and there was only that one), I could tell dozens of stories with different endings.

Another reason to stay where you are is that distressed and semi-distressed companies generally offer more interesting legal work.

Living (and working) in interesting times may sound like that famous ancient curse, but consider this. It is not bad for your career to have worked on interesting, challenging, and high stakes matters, whether you stay in the company you help to save, or whether you have to move on later in your career. You get noticed more. You widen your portfolio of skills.

For example, at International Harvester, I was hired to do labor and employment work. Almost all of my first assignments were union arbitrations. I had a good won/loss record. I enjoyed the work.

About a year after I joined the Company, I got a call from a legal recruiter. It was simply an exploratory call. He wanted to introduce himself and test my willingness to join another company. He asked me about my work. I told him about doing employment litigation and union arbitrations. He asked me if I liked the work. I said I did. Then he asked me about my ultimate career goals. At the time I didn't have any particular "ultimate career goals". But I knew what headhunters wanted to hear, and so I said I wanted to become a General Counsel. Safe thing to say.

I've never forgotten what he said next.

"Then what are you doing in labor and employment law?"

"Well, I like it. And it's important work." My voice trailed off. What else was there to say?

"Look, Steve, if you want to become a General Counsel, you need to expand your portfolio beyond labor and employment. To borrow an expression, you need to follow the money. That means finance and securities law."

"Why is that?"

"Because corporations are about money. And, aside from sales, there are only two ways for a public corporation to raise money. One is to borrow it, either in private or public transactions. That's finance. The other is to sell stock. That's securities. You need to work in finance and securities. That's where General Counsels come from."

I thanked him and said I'd think about what he said. I must have made a weak impression on him because I never heard from him again. But he had made a strong impression on me.

I didn't become a finance and securities lawyer the next day. But slowly I began to do other things beyond labor and employment. As it happened, right around the time of that conversation, International Harvester Company was scrambling to generate cash. The scramble eventually resulted in the Company's exit from its founding farm equipment business. But for the several years preceding that big sale, there were multiple smaller sales of so-called non-core assets.

As a result, the Company suddenly had a need for lawyering work on divestitures. I became deeply involved in selling things. Real estate. Non-core subsidiaries. Idle factories. You name it, I helped to sell it. Almost overnight, I became an experienced deal lawyer. Which led to other assignments. If I had continued to do union arbitrations for my entire career, the headhunter's warning likely would have come true. I probably would not have become General Counsel.

But if you are still thinking about making the move to another corporation, here is one more thing to consider. Many of your colleagues are thinking the same thing. As you debate whether to stay or go, some of your colleagues have already made up their minds. And their departure can open up opportunities for you. I got my first sizable promotion at International Harvester when a more senior lawyer left the Company. He went to Dart & Kraft. In the interest of full disclosure, I believe he was happy and successful at Dart & Kraft. He worked there for many years until his retirement.

Meanwhile, back at International Harvester, I got his job.

He was the finance and securities lawyer.

CHAPTER 8

Don't Act Like You're Smarter Than Your Clients – Even If You Think You Are

When I was in law school, I took a course on Wills and Trusts taught by a crusty old professor who was a classic know-it-all.

One evening one of the students mentioned something about estate planning services offered by insurance agents. I went to law school at night, so it's possible the student was himself an insurance agent by day and a law student at night. It wouldn't have mattered to our professor. Tact definitely was not his strong suit. In his gravelly voice, he practically shouted, "Why on earth would you listen to anything an insurance agent says? Do you know what the definition of an insurance agent is? He's a guy who got a low score on the LSAT!"

It was one of the first of many incidents when I encountered lawyers who thought they were smarter than everybody else.

In the course of my career I encountered more than one lawyer who had a disdain for non-lawyers. It may be excusable. We lawyers almost always know the law better than our clients. That can lead to the self-delusion that we know *everything* better than our clients.

But it is a dangerous attitude for an in-house lawyer. For two pretty important reasons.

First, if you think you are smarter than your client, the chances are good you're wrong. Managers and executives in most corporations, the people who are your clients, don't get their jobs by being dumb. Exceptions may prove the rule, but the rule is still there. One way to prove it is to ask yourself how easily you would be able to do the work your clients do. Over time the experiences of working in-house teach you that your clients usually are just as smart as you are, if not smarter. You will learn just as much from them as they learn from you.

Second, no matter how clever you think you are in hiding it, the clients will know it if you have the attitude that, to borrow a phrase, you are the smartest guy in the room. And guess what? They won't like it. And given the fact that in-house lawyers only really have one client, your attitude will end up costing you influence, opportunities and perhaps even your job. So when someone in management uses the word "irregardless" in a meeting, let it go. Not everyone was a liberal arts major.

I was humbled by the superior intelligence of my clients so often that my examples could fill a book all by themselves. To save myself too much humiliation, I picked out two examples for this particular rule. Here they are.

Someone once sent me that board game that is on the table at all Cracker Barrel restaurants. It was sort of an inside joke, but that's beside the point. If you've never played it, the game consists of a triangular playing board that contains 15 holes arranged in five rows, with 5 holes in one row, 4 holes in the next row, then 3, then 2 and the last row has one. The game board has 14 removable tees that fit into the holes. One hole is empty. The object of the game is to pick up a tee and "jump" an adjacent tee and remove it, until there is only one tee left on the board. You can only jump a tee that is next to the jumping tee.

I kept the game sitting on the conference table that was in my office. I confess that I sometimes played it during especially boring conference calls. The back side of the game board has the scoring rules. It informs you that if you succeed in jumping all the tees and leave only one on the board, you are "a genius". If you leave 3 tees on the board at the end of the game, you are "just plain dumb". Whenever I played, I left 3 tees on the board. Sometimes 4.

One day my boss, who was the CEO, dropped by my office. He noticed the game. He had never played it. He asked me to explain it to him. I did. Long before his CEO days, my boss had been an engineer. He took a minute to look at the board. Then he started playing.

On his first try, he left two pieces on the board. On his second try, only the second time he had ever played, he left one tee on the board, a perfect score. He had earned the "Genius" title. To make my point even stronger about never thinking you are smarter than your clients, I asked him to explain how he did it. He told me. In some detail. I thanked him. Our meeting ended. He went back to his office.

As soon as he left, I picked up the game and played it, trying to follow the winning strategy that the CEO had just explained to me.

I left 3 tees.

I got another great reminder of the rule that clients are just as smart as I, just in different ways, the first time I went to Navistar's Springfield, Ohio plant. The Springfield plant was the place where the Company assembled trucks and school buses.

I can't tell you much about how trucks are made. But I can tell you how the assembly process begins. They lay two long steel beams on the assembly line. These are called frame rails. Then they start attaching stuff to the frame rails. At the end of the assembly line, it's a truck.

On the day of my first visit to Springfield, my tour started with a look at this first step. I watched the frame rails being laid on the assembly line. Then a machine poked holes in the steel. They called this part "frame rail piercing". It was an interesting process to watch. The piercing machine actually penetrated the steel all the way through, leaving a round hole in the frame rail about the size of a quarter, and in the process, pushing out a small cylindrical piece of steel that fell into a large container underneath the assembly line.

As I stood watching the process, I casually reached into the container that held the small plugs of steel that had been pushed out by the frame rail piercer. I picked one up. I started to ask, "What do you do with all these piercings?"

But I didn't get to finish the question. Those of you who were engineering students before you became lawyers already know why. For the rest of you, the reason I couldn't finish my question was because I was holding an extremely hot piece of steel. The force of pushing those steel plugs out of the frame rail produced a tremendous amount of heat. And I was holding it in my hand. At least for a moment, until I shouted in pain and dropped it.

In fairness to the manufacturing managers who were showing me around, they tried to stop me before I picked up the steel piece. I was just too quick for them.

As I said, I had lots of other opportunities to learn that I wasn't smarter than my clients. But the frame rail story is the one that stayed with me. I guess you could say it was seared into my memory.

CHAPTER 9

Press the Delete Key at the End – Not When You Think You're at the End

The world of in-house lawyering can be pretty fast-paced. It's a world of skimming written articles looking for the important points, skipping lengthy text to read just the conclusions, providing advice in real time with limited opportunity for reflection. And when we're done, we press the Delete key. We delete emails. We delete instant messages. After we've given our off-the-cuff advice, we end the meeting and go on to the next thing, which is its own form of hitting the Delete key. In short, we're always in a hurry. And, like they say, speed kills.

People who give advice often say that one of the best things anyone who uses email can do is to pause and reread the emails they write in anger before pushing the send button. It's good advice, I guess. But it requires taking the time to do that reread. Although I think if you're the type of person who would write an email that, upon reflection, shouldn't be sent, you're probably the type of person who will end up sending it anyway.

My rule has to do with when you're the message receiver, not the message sender. It's important to be thorough enough that you know you've gotten not just the gist of the message, but the entire message. Reading the message start to finish, or listening to the message start to finish, sooner or later will be important. I learned this rule the hard way.

Before text messaging and emailing, there was voicemail. Voicemail capability arrived at International Harvester in the 1980s.

I remember going to a training session on how voicemail worked and what it could do. There were two ways you could send a voicemail message.

One way was the old-fashioned way. Dial the recipient's phone number. If the person doesn't answer, wait for the beep and then leave your message.

The other way was to go into your own voicemail box. I forget exactly how you did that. I think you dialed some universal phone number and entered a code. Then you pressed 1 and recorded your message. When you were finished, you entered the phone number of the person to whom you were sending the message, and then pressed 1 (or maybe 2) to send it. The beauty of this second method was that you didn't have to actually call the person and risk the possibility that they would answer their phone and you'd have to talk to them, which would take up more of your precious time.

I attended the voicemail training with a Labor Relations manager, who was nearing retirement, and who had had enough telephone conversations in his career to last two lifetimes. When he learned which buttons he needed to push to send voicemails without having to actually talk with the recipient, he turned to me, and with a broad smile said, "Steve this is the last time you and I will be talking to each other live and in person. I guess this is goodbye." We laughed. He was kidding. At least I think he was.

I knew another employee who attended the same voicemail training session and afterward returned all of his calls by sending voicemail messages. As he explained it, it gave him the opportunity to get credit for returning the call by leaving a voicemail message, bought time so that the caller's original reason for calling him might go away, and relieved him of the need to have lengthy back and forth conversations. He called it "win-win".

Our first voicemail system allowed up to five minutes of recording time per message. At that time my job required me to communicate often with our CEO. He travelled a lot. I ended up leaving him a lot of voicemails. This particular CEO had a pet peeve about voicemails that he openly shared with everyone. He hated long ones. He let everyone know that he expected all messages in his voicemail box to be no more than one minute in length. If the voicemail messages were longer than that, the sender would hear from him, and the feedback could be scathing. As is the case with most CEOs, he got dozens of voicemail messages every day, and the extra-long ones were that much more of an irritation.

For some reason I had a hard time meeting the one-minute rule. The beep would sound, I would leave my message for him, and then press the button that allowed me to listen to my own message before sending it. After it replayed, the recorded voice told me the length of the message. Too often, mine would be longer than a minute, sometimes substantially longer.

So I would have to push the button that erased my first message, push the button that allowed me to re-record, and then try again. Sometimes I needed five or six tries before I got below one minute. It required a lot of skill. I learned to talk faster. And I eliminated unnecessary phrases like "I'm leaving you this voicemail message because...", which saved a full 3 seconds. Believe me, I've timed it. And I trained myself to omit information that was not critical, which I covered by ending every message with "Call me if you'd like additional information."

In later years I was sometimes complimented for my skill at providing concise "executive summaries". Whenever I received that compliment, it always made me smile, thinking about how one of the ways I taught conciseness to myself years before was by re-recording all of those voicemail messages. Training comes in many forms.

While my system for re-recording my voicemail messages kept me in the good graces of the CEO, my own impatience at listening to the voicemails sent to me once got me into hot water with that same CEO. Hence the rule.

I had a secretary who, to put it mildly, had very minimal skills when it came to leaving voicemail messages. For one thing, she talked so slowly that it was agonizing to have to listen to her messages. I could fix that by pressing the button that speeded up her voice. It was sort of like listening to a 33 1/3 rpm record album at 45 rpms.

But what I couldn't fix was that every time she left a voicemail message, she repeated the entire message. It would go like this. She would slowly say her message, and then at some point she would say, "So like I said..." and then she would say the whole thing a second time. She did it every time.

I thought I had figured out a good system. When I listened to her message, I waited for the "so like I said" phrase. I knew that meant she was about to start over and say the same message a second time. When I heard her say, "so like I said," I pressed the star key followed by the Number 3 key, and that deleted the message. I got accustomed to never listening to her messages from start to finish. My system seemed to work.

But one time, my secretary left me a voicemail that wasn't like the others. It started like they all did. "I'm calling to let you know that I finished work on that project you assigned to me and I left it on your desk. You can let me know tomorrow whether you have any changes to make to it. So like I said..." And that's when I pressed the delete buttons, certain that I'd heard the whole thing.

But here's what I'd missed.

After "So like I said," came the usual repeating of the message. "I finished work on that project you assigned to me and I left it on your desk. You can let me know tomorrow whether you have any changes to make to it." But then the message continued. "Oh, and I just remembered, the CEO called. He has some questions for you and he wants you to call him as soon as you can. So like I said, the CEO has questions for you and he wants you to call him as soon as you can."

Of course, I didn't hear that part. I'd deleted the message after her first "so like I said." I never thought about the possibility that there might be more than one "so like I said". When she asked me the next day whether I had called the CEO, I had no idea what she was talking about.

When I finally connected with the CEO, he was not pleased that it had taken so long for me to call. I briefly thought about telling him the "so like I said" story. But I knew it would take longer than a minute to tell it.

So like I said. Press the Delete key at the end, not when you think you're at the end.

CHAPTER 10

Ask The Right Number of Questions

In-house lawyers are often in a hurry, in no small part because our clients are always in a hurry. They want immediate answers. They need immediate answers.

A seldom told secret of in-house lawyering success is that what we learned in law school, or as a new associate in a law firm, namely, that it's a perfectly fine answer to say to a client, "I don't know, but I'll find out", doesn't really work in the in-house environment. It is one of the significant differences between law firm practice and in-house practice.

The in-house lawyer's clients are business people. They operate by the 80/20 rule. The 80/20 rule says that you shouldn't wait to act until you know 100% of what you need to know and are 100% certain about the action you plan to take. It will take too long. You'll miss the opportunity. Take action when your knowledge level is at 80%. You can always adjust as you learn more.

Business people who operate according to that rule are comfortable with others following it as well. As a successful General Counsel once summed it up for me, "The clients want your best answer today, not your perfect answer next week." In other words, they are comfortable with your answer if you are 80% certain you're right, because they have to learn to be comfortable with the same level of certainty in their work. And you need to remember that seeking your legal advice is only one of a number of boxes that your client is checking off as he or she works toward a decision point.

So if your answer is "I don't know, but I'll find out," what happens is your client puts your non-advice in the 20 part of the 80/20 rule, which is not a good or helpful thing.

For in-house lawyers, the trick in succeeding in the 80/20 world of business is to be comfortable giving your legal advice when you're 80% sure of your answer, but for your legal advice to be right way more than 80% of the time. Which sounds just about as hard as it is. How to do it?

The best way I know is to make sure you are as informed as possible before you form your legal opinion. We all learned in law school how to brief a case. It always starts with the facts. After law school, we all quickly learn that in applying the law to the facts, it is critical to get the facts right. And to do that, you need to ask a lot of questions. Clients almost always are comfortable answering questions. They want to be helpful. They like talking about their work. And the best of them know that your advice will be better if they provide you with the facts you need.

But in the end, it's up to you to know what questions to ask. And to know when you've asked all the questions you need to ask.

As one of the Company's lawyers, I represented management at a lot of labor arbitrations. If one of the unions representing our employees filed a grievance alleging that management had violated the collective bargaining contract, an arbitration hearing was the way to finally resolve the grievance if the parties had not otherwise agreed to a resolution.

Arbitrations were like informal trials. We often held arbitration hearings in hotel conference rooms. The arbitrator sat at the head of the table and acted the role of judge. Union representatives sat on one side of the table and management representatives sat on the other side. Documents were presented to the arbitrator. Witnesses were questioned and cross-examined. I did the questioning on behalf of management.

I handled an arbitration once where I asked one question too few as I prepared for the hearing.

The facts seemed simple. An employee at one of our manufacturing plants was stealing hand tools. The area where he worked was always needing replacement tools. Plant Security had suspected he was taking hand tools home with him for some time. They watched him leave at the end of his shift. He went to his car. The Plant Security officers followed him. After he got in, they approached his car. The front seat was loaded with hand tools. Wrenches, screw drivers, hammers. It was clear he was the thief. They fired him.

The union filed a grievance. I represented the Company at the arbitration hearing. As part of my preparation, I interviewed the Plant Security officers who followed the employee into the parking lot and found the tools in his car. And I interviewed the Human Resources manager who handled the employee's termination.

I asked the HR manager about the tools. I asked, "How do you know the tools were Company tools? How did you know they weren't his own personal tools?"

The HR manager replied, "The tools we found were the kind of tools used by the workers in this employee's assigned area. They were the same kind of tools we'd had to replace when they were reported as lost. And one more thing. We put a stamp on all of our hand tools. Every hand tool is stamped with an 'IH' symbol on it. IH stands for International Harvester."

"And did the tools you found in the employee's car have the IH stamp on them?

"They did."

I couldn't think of any more questions. That sounded like all I needed. I was ready for the arbitration hearing.

I remember how confident I felt as the hearing began The general wisdom about arbitrations with unions was that it was a little easier for management to win a case involving the interpretation of the collective bargaining contract, and a little harder for management to win a case involving disciplinary action taken against an employee, and even harder when the discipline was employment termination. Arbitrators tended to frown on employee terminations unless they were completely satisfied that the Company had good cause for the termination.

But my case was about stealing Company property, and good cause was established by the fact that we caught the employee with the stolen goods in his possession. I had a sure winner.

The union's lawyer's first witness was the chairman of the local bargaining unit. After the witness was sworn, the lawyer pulled a bunch of hand tools out of his briefcase and handed them to the union chairman. He asked, "Do you recognize these tools?"

"Yes", said the bargaining unit chairman.

"Do these tools belong to you?"

"Yes."

"And do you see the IH stamped on each of these tools?"

"Yes, I do."

The lawyer asked, "Can you explain how these tools can belong to you when they have the IH stamp on them?"

"Sure", said the bargaining unit chairman, and he looked over at me with a "gotcha" smirk. "When hand tools like these begin to wear out, the Company sells them in bulk to a hardware store down the street from the plant. The hardware store resells them to their retail customers. I bought these tools at that hardware store."

"Your witness," said the union's lawyer.

I skipped cross-examination.

The union's next witness was the terminated employee. The union's lawyer asked him where he'd gotten the tools that the Plant Security officers observed in his car.

He said, "I bought them at the hardware store down the street from the plant."

I also skipped that cross-examination.

I asked the arbitrator for a brief recess and huddled with the Human Resources manager. He confirmed everything we'd just heard. Both he and the Plant Security people were so certain that the employee was a thief that the alternative explanation hadn't occurred to them. I wanted to blame him for what was sure to be a loss. But I knew that it was on me. I had asked one question too few.

Most rules have exceptions and this one is no different. If you never stop asking questions, if question asking becomes your way of avoiding ever reaching a conclusion and giving your advice, you are doing it wrong.

I worked with an in-house lawyer who worked hard to avoid ever having to take a position. His method was to ask questions, and then more questions. I believe he thought that he was demonstrating to the client how smart he was, that he was asking them questions that they hadn't thought of. What he accomplished instead was that fewer and fewer clients sought out his advice at all. It helped to end his career sooner than he'd planned.

Think of it like that story of Goldilocks. Too few questions is bad. Too many questions is bad. In the middle is just right.

Any questions?

CHAPTER 11

Follow the Advice of Others – But Make Your Own Decisions

I like benchmarking. I didn't always. It was an acquired skill.

Most lawyers, including the in-house ones, go through their own know-it-all phase. For most of us, it starts sometime after we pass the bar exam, and if we are lucky it ends soon after we commit our first major screw up.

Using what others have already developed is the lifeblood of a lot of our work. For example, not long after I became Corporate Secretary at Navistar, the Securities and Exchange Commission adopted new rules for reporting the ownership, purchase and sale of a public company's securities by its significant shareholders, executive officers, and directors. I prepared a 20 minute presentation to our Board of Directors explaining the new rules, and the procedures the directors would have to follow to comply with them. I did a good job. I went through the fine points of how to prepare and file Form 3 (initial ownership report), Form 4 (purchase or sale) and Form 5 (year-end compliance). I even passed out the forms the directors could use in preparing their reports. Well done, Steve, I told myself.

After the Board meeting, one of the directors, a very kind man who was a university professor, came up to me and said, "Good report, Steve. But I'm on another board, and their corporate secretary had us sign powers of attorney so that he can file the forms for us. We just call him to let him know whenever we're going to do a transaction in the company's stock and he does the rest. Here's his name and number. You should call him."

I was lucky that he was such a nice man. He didn't call me out in front of the other directors. I have encountered directors since that time who would not have hesitated to tell me in the middle of my report that I was an idiot for suggesting that they file the SEC reports themselves.

I checked around, a process also known as benchmarking, and I discovered that the director was right. And in the process, I found a much better way to do what I thought had to be done by the directors themselves.

Benchmarking. Not just for plagiarists. But for all of us.

The tricky part about following this rule is knowing when to follow it and when not to. Benchmarking can never substitute for thinking it through and making your own decision.

On more than once occasion my corporate clients pushed back when I told them that something they wanted to do wasn't permissible. They said that one or more of our competitors, or suppliers, or customers, were already doing what I was telling them they couldn't do. Pushback like that always makes you slow down and recheck your own advice, which is the right thing to do. But thankfully I never changed my advice and agreed on a course of action just because some other company was doing it. And more than once I had the private satisfaction of later reading about the other company's misfortune of being sued, or even prosecuted, for doing what I concluded Navistar couldn't do.

I say that I was privately satisfied because an obvious rule of being an in-house lawyer is never to tell the client "I told you so". There are two reasons for never saying "I told you so." One, the good clients usually remember that you told them so and they don't need to be reminded. And two, if you remind them that you told them so, what they also will be reminded of is that you made their job harder, because they had to come up with an alternate solution when you vetoed their first choice.

The best example I can offer for making your own decisions occurred in Pocahontas, Iowa. Pocahontas is a town in the middle of the state of Iowa, about 40 miles from Fort Dodge. The population of Pocahontas is a little under 2,000.

International Harvester owned a subsidiary called Iowa Industrial Hydraulics. It was located in Pocahontas. The workers at Iowa Industrial Hydraulics were members of a union.

One year, the Company laid off all of the union workers just before the annual Christmas holiday shutdown. The collective bargaining agreement said that you didn't get holiday pay if the holiday occurred while you were on layoff. So none of the workers received holiday pay for the Christmas and New Year holidays.

The union filed a grievance. I was assigned to represent management at the arbitration hearing.

On a warm summer day I took a plane from Chicago to Fort Dodge, Iowa, rented a car, drove to Pocahontas, checked into the Big Chief Motel, had dinner at the Princess Cafe, then had breakfast the next morning at the Princess Cafe, then went to the courthouse where the arbitration hearing took place.

The Pocahontas County Courthouse was an old building. Very stately looking. The inside of the courtroom reminded me of the courtroom scene in the movie, "To Kill a Mockingbird." It made me feel a little like Atticus Finch.

The other thing that made me feel like I'd walked onto the set of "To Kill a Mockingbird" was that the place was packed! Every seat was occupied. I think there were people standing in the back. It looked like the whole town had turned out to watch the proceedings. All 2,000 of them!

I was accompanied by one of the Company's Labor Relations managers. As we sat down, he whispered to me, "The first thing you should do is ask the arbitrator to clear the courtroom."

"Why?" I asked.

"Most of the people in this room are either employees, or family members of employees, who didn't get that holiday pay we're arguing they shouldn't have gotten. What if they decide to lynch you and me?"

"Are you serious?"

"All you have to do is make a motion asking the arbitrator to exclude anyone from the hearing who isn't a witness," he said. "I've seen it done lots of times. If you had time to do a benchmarking study, you'd see that it's a best practice. It always works. The arbitrator absolutely will do it. Everyone will have to leave the courtroom."

I thought about it for a moment. And then I made my decision. Benchmarking be damned, at least this time.

"I'm not going to do it," I said. "For one thing, they don't look like an angry mob to me. And besides, what if the arbitrator grants my motion and they refuse to leave? What then? Do we call the cops? How big do you figure the Pocahontas, Iowa police force is? And whose side will the cops be on? And if the arbitrator denies my motion, he won't like it that I even asked in the first place."

So I played to a packed house. The arbitrator took his seat on the judge's bench. I delivered my opening argument. The union's representative did the same. We examined and cross-examined our first witness. About an hour after the hearing started, we took a break. From the judge's bench where he was sitting, the arbitrator addressed the audience, and what he said made it clear that any motion to eject the audience would have been a bad idea.

"I'm so glad you are all here," the arbitrator said. "This is a great opportunity for you to see the arbitration part of the collective bargaining process in action." He then asked if anybody had any questions for him! And several people did. They were polite. They raised their hands. They asked thoughtful questions.

We didn't get lynched.

As a postscript, I can say that, unlike Atticus Finch in "To Kill a Mockingbird", I won my case. Although in fairness, his case was harder.

CHAPTER 12

Be Concise

I was sitting in our Friday morning staff meeting. The president of the Company was running the meeting. He turned to the head of Human Resources and said, "I noticed that one of the two elevators is out of service. Do you know when it will be fixed?"

The HR manager responded. "I talked to the landlord. He is aware of the problem. He has called the repair service."

The president said, "So when will it be fixed?"

"The repair people say that they have to do some diagnostic work before they can get the elevator back in service."

"So when will it be fixed?"

"Once the repair people determine which parts they will need, they will order the parts and when the parts arrive, they will work on fixing the problem."

By this time, the president was visibly irritated. "All I'm asking is when will it be fixed? Do you know?" he asked in a loud voice.

"I don't know."

My friend in Human Resources had just failed the "Be concise" test.

My first boss at International Harvester Company was a fantastic lawyer. He'd been working in the Company's Law Department for about 20 years. I learned so much from him. He had a great analytical mind. He was the best listener I ever worked with. And he had a scarily accurate memory. He remembered file numbers and witness names years after the files had closed and been shipped to the warehouse.

But his best skill may have been his ability to be concise. Although when he combined it with his irreverent sense of humor, it sometimes got him into trouble. Once, his boss was escorting a visitor from another company through our Law Department. Visitor in tow, my boss' boss stopped at my boss' office door and said, "Would you take a minute and explain to our visitor what you do here?" To which my boss sarcastically replied, "Why don't I take a minute and a half and tell him what we both do?"

He could dish out shots like that, but he could also take them. Once I was in his office when a new lawsuit arrived on his desk. He decided to hire his favorite outside counsel, who later became my favorite. Their conversation was short.

My boss said, "We've just been sued by a former employee. I want you to represent us. It's a simple case. In fact, my dog could win this case."

The outside counsel, who had known my boss for a long time, replied, "Then hire your dog."

"Touche," my boss laughed. "I'll send you the summons and complaint today."

My first boss excelled in a lot of things, but when it came to conciseness, especially when talking with our clients, he was the best I ever saw. He never left anything important out. He never put anything unimportant in. He never said anything extra.

Early in my career at the Company, he asked me to research a legal question to help one of our clients decide on a course of action. When I was done, I went into his office. For about ten minutes, I told him about the cases I'd read, how some of the decisions would favor one course of action, and others would favor another. I explained how the facts tended to influence the holdings. I mentioned the dissenting points of view in the cases. I compared and contrasted the outcomes in the cases decided in the federal circuit where we were located vs. the outcomes in other circuits. He never spoke while I talked, just intently listened. That was his way. I am convinced that, if he had been called upon to do so, he could have repeated everything I said word-for-word. His memory and listening skills were that good.

When I was done, he picked up his phone and called the client. I listened while he summarized everything I had just told him. I had taken 10 minutes. He took about 30 seconds, maybe not even that long. And his summary was perfect. I sat in awe. I thought to myself, "I want to be able to do that."

I never achieved his skill level. But I worked on it. And I got better. Ten years later I was the Company's Corporate Secretary. My job included working on letters to the Board of Directors. More than once, I edited three and four page Board reports that featured extraneous information written in rambling prose. When I was done with my editing, the final report was less than one page long. I always made sure that the reports contained everything the directors needed in order to do their jobs and make their decisions. Like my first boss, I never left anything important out. And I tried never to say anything extra.

Clients appreciate conciseness. It comes as a surprise to some in-house lawyers, but generally, clients want an answer. They don't want to know, and truthfully don't need to know, everything that you know. Sometimes you can even hear it in the way they ask their questions.

Sometime after I became General Counsel, I attended a meeting called by the Company's CEO. I sat in the conference room with the CEO and six or seven other top executives. The CEO described to us a decision he had to make. He asked for input. We gave it. Like all corporate meetings, this one went on for a while. I have often said that the minimum length of time for any corporate meeting can be calculated by counting the number of people in the room and multiplying that number by 5 minutes, since each person will talk for at least that long if given the chance. Finally, our advice had been given. Not everyone agreed on what decision should be made.

The CEO looked around the table and said, "OK, thanks for the input. Now I want to go around the table and get a simple yes or no." One by one, each person offered their vote. And every person managed to say some condensed version of their viewpoint in addition to yes or no. When the CEO came to me, I thought about how my first boss would have handled the moment. "No," I said. That was all I said. The CEO laughed and said, "How about that? The lawyer was the one who talked the least." I'm pretty sure he meant it as a compliment. Pretty sure.

On the subject of CEOs and conciseness, here is something I learned about CEOs. They are busy. Their calendars are full all day long. The chances are good that while you are meeting with the CEO, the people who will be meeting with him or her next will be sitting in the waiting area right outside the CEO's office. And while you are waxing eloquent and demonstrating what a great lawyer you are, the CEO likely is wondering whether he or she will have time to go to the bathroom before the next meeting starts. I tried to make it a habit of finishing up at least 5 minutes before my scheduled meeting time ended.

I once read about a Chicago alderman who sat in the City Council for many years and never once made a speech. In fact, the record showed that he had never spoken at all at any City Council meeting. He must have been a good alderman because the people in his ward kept re-electing him. Finally, after decades in the position, the silent alderman retired. After his last City Council meeting, where he once again did not speak, a reporter interviewed him and mentioned the fact that the alderman had never once spoken at a City Council meeting. The reporter asked him why. The alderman replied, "I believe that you should never pass up an opportunity to keep your mouth shut."

How concise should you be? Of course, like most things, it depends on the circumstances and your audience. But keep in mind that your clients want an answer, not a lecture, and certainly not a speech. My advice is to try for just a little more verbosity than that silent Chicago alderman. But not too much more.

CHAPTER 13

Know Who's on the Other Side of the Table

There are so many relationships going on at your company that it can be hard to keep track of them. For example, someone once asked me to file a lawsuit against a trucking company we had hired to transport some material for us. Some of our material was damaged during the shipment. We blamed the trucking company. The trucking company said it wasn't their fault and refused to pay. The corporate transportation manager told me the story. It was a pretty clear case of liability. I filed the lawsuit.

Within several days, a very upset sales executive showed up in my office. "Steve," he said, "did you file a lawsuit against the XYZ Trucking Company?"

"Yes," I told him. "They damaged some of our stuff and they're refusing to pay for the damage. I've reviewed the file. We're right. I expect to win."

"That may be," he replied, "but I just got off the phone with one of our best dealers, who told me XYZ is one of his top customers, but won't be much longer if we continue this lawsuit."

"But it's a near certain win," I said, somewhat lamely.

"A near certain win is our sale to this customer of hundreds of trucks per year. Compared to the value of that relationship, the money you're trying to collect is a tiny amount. Please call your outside counsel and drop the lawsuit today."

The sales executive was right. It was a lesson that stayed with me.

I learned a lot about the value of knowing who is on the other side of the table. But my best teachers for that lesson were not Company employees. They were union leaders, especially those who worked for the UAW.

My dad worked for International Harvester in the mid-1950s. Here's how he got the job. His mother lived in Rock Island, Illinois. Her house was about three blocks from the Farmall plant. Rock Island is a hilly city. You could stand at the edge of my grandmother's back yard and look down toward the Mississippi river below and see the plant. My grandmother worked as a waitress in a diner at the train station that was next to the International Harvester plant. She knew the plant was hiring, and she encouraged my dad to apply.

My dad moved his family, including his three year old son (me), from Chicago to Rock Island and got a job at the plant. He worked nights. His job involved sharpening tools for the day shift. He only stayed until the first big layoff. With a young family, he couldn't afford to be out of work waiting to be recalled from layoff, and so we moved back to Chicago less than a year later.

Almost thirty years later, not long after I joined the Law Department at International Harvester, I was sitting in a very large conference room. It was on the first floor of World Headquarters. The occasion was the opening of collective bargaining negotiations with the United Auto Workers. There was a great deal of ceremony involved in the commencement of labor contract negotiations in those days.

All of the union representatives who attended the negotiations were seated on one side of a very long table. Management representatives sat on the opposite side. The Company's head of Labor Relations sat on the management side, in the middle of the table. Opposite him was the UAW's chief negotiator. The other UAW representatives at the table included bargaining unit chairmen from each of the plants. There were a lot of them. Management didn't have enough Human Resources managers to equal the number of UAW attendees at the opening session. So they asked some of the Company's lawyers, including me, to sit on the management side of the table to balance things out.

I took a seat at the end of the table opposite the chairman of the UAW local at the Rock Island Farmall plant. As the ceremony unfolded, complete with photos being taken of the symbolic handshake between the top negotiators, I began to notice that the Farmall bargaining unit chairman was looking straight at me in a very curious way. I wondered if something was wrong. Had I sat in the wrong spot? Did he have a grievance he wanted to discuss?

The ceremony ended and everyone got up to leave. I noticed the Farmall bargaining unit chairman was coming around the table toward me. He said, "Pardon me, but I think I know you." Then he shook his head and said, "No, that can't be it." He stood thinking for a moment, and then asked, "Did you ever work at Farmall"?

I said, "No. My dad worked there. But that was 30 years ago."

He brightened and asked, "What shift?"

"I don't know for sure," I said, "but I know he worked nights."

"That's it," he said triumphantly. "He was a tool sharpener. He would have been about the same age you are now." I told him he was right.

That story taught me a great lesson about union officials, how well they paid attention to, and knew, the men and women who were on the other side of their table, namely, the people they represented. The people who elected them. UAW leaders often referred to "the men and women who I am honored to represent". They said it the same way, using the same words, every time. I thought it must have been something they had to memorize as part of their training. But however they learned it, over time I came to see that most of them meant it.

I also learned that knowing who they were dealing with made them better negotiators than the majority of people they negotiated against. I tried to learn from their example.

By the time I was General Counsel, I had learned the value of knowing as much as possible about who was on the other side of the table. The lawyers on my staff, especially the ones who handled lawsuits, became accustomed to answering the questions I asked about the matters they were handling. Who is our opponent? What is their motivation? Are they angry? Are they trying to save face? How much money have they spent on their lawyers so far? If we plan to settle the case, what is the best settlement currency from the other side's point of view? Money? A new business relationship with our Company? Our agreement to drop our counterclaim?

Some people learn that it's important to know who is on the other side of the table. And some people don't.

In the 1980s our Engine Engineering department developed a great new diesel engine. Reflecting its displacement, it was called the 6.9 liter engine. We sold so many of them to one of the auto companies for use in its heavy duty pickup trucks that by the middle of the decade, if you said the words "Six Nine" at the Company, everybody knew what you were talking about.

But we faced a challenge before production of the 6.9 liter engine could begin. The challenge was money. In the early 1980s at International Harvester Company, there wasn't a lot of it. And there was tooling and assembly equipment that had to be bought. Expensive stuff.

Our Treasury Department looked for financing sources and found that there weren't a lot of borrowing options available to us. Finally they found the president of a German bank who was interested enough to come to the U.S. for our borrowing pitch.

The banker toured the Company's engine production plant in Indianapolis, Indiana where the 6.9 liter engine was going to be manufactured. He also toured our other engine plant in Melrose Park, Illinois. Then we had a series of meetings at the Company's World Headquarters in Chicago. I attended those meetings.

For many of us on the negotiating team, it was a cultural challenge to try to build a working relationship. We were all midwestern American metal benders. We were talking to the president of a bank, and a German bank at that. Even small talk during our sessions seemed strained.

One afternoon the small talk turned to personal backgrounds. How long had the German banker been in the banking business? What had he done before working in banking? The banker told us that during the war, World War II, he had been in the German army and had been the commander of a panzer unit.

I was sitting next to the Finance Manager from our Treasury Department. He suddenly brightened and said, "What a small world! At our other Engine plant, the one in Melrose Park, Illinois, we manufactured engines that went into U.S. medium bombers during World War II. Maybe one of our engines was in a bomber that dropped bombs on your tank during the war!"

I don't know if it was meant to be funny. Or if our Finance Manager was just desperate for something relevant to say. At any rate, the banker coolly replied, "Perhaps". And the meeting continued.

I'm sure that episode had nothing to do with the outcome. But in the end, we had to find the money somewhere else.

CHAPTER 14

Always Let the Client Be the Good Guy

Before I joined the Law Department of International Harvester Company, I practiced law in Chicago for almost four years. Chicago is a big place, with lots of lawyers and even more clients. One result of the work I did, in the place where I did it, was that I never dealt with anyone more than once. As a result, all of my encounters with counsel for the other side were transactions. All of my encounters with their clients were transactions. All of my encounters with judges were transactions. No relationships, just transactions.

But life in-house is different.

My very first assignment at International Harvester was to represent the Company at a labor arbitration hearing in Baltimore. My client was the Labor Relations manager. (Even though our client always was the corporation, we referred to the business managers for whom we worked as clients). My opponent was an attorney for the Teamsters union. Her client was the union's business agent.

The issue in the hearing was a contractual dispute concerning employee benefits. I don't remember the details. I do remember that the union's attorney and I argued a lot, objected to various pieces of evidence, and vigorously cross-examined each other's witnesses. The union's attorney was quite animated in presenting the merits of her case, and so was I. I was operating in the mode I had developed in private practice. I would never see any of these people again.

The hearing ended. Then something caught my attention. As we were getting ready to leave the hearing room, my client, the Labor Relations manager, went to the other side of the table and shook hands with the union's business agent. The two men had a friendly discussion. They laughed at each other's jokes. They each wished the other good luck.

On the ride to the airport, I mentioned my observation to my client and asked him if the union business agent was a personal friend. "No," said my client, "but I will be seeing him again in a couple of weeks to discuss another grievance that's pending. And negotiations for the next collective bargaining agreement will be coming up soon. So it's important for me to have a good relationship with him."

I was struck by the obviousness of what he said. I was also struck by the fact that it was a first of its kind experience for me. In private practice I had never been rude to opponents, but I had treated them like, well, opponents. I said, "Well, in that case, do you think I came on too strong in the arbitration? Do I owe someone an apology?" He shook his head. "No, you did just what I wanted you to do, just what you're supposed to do. My job is relationship building. In this setting, yours isn't."

In-house lawyers have to accept the critical fact that if anyone is going to be the bad guy, it has to be them. The clients aren't made for the task. There are several reasons for this.

First, the clients you work with, at least the ones who are successful, generally become successful, and stay successful, by building value through building relationships. In fact, the most successful CEOs with whom I worked spent almost all of their time building relationships. Relationships with customers, with shareholders, with the members of their Board of Directors, with the media, with investment analysts, with suppliers and distributors, and with their own management team and the employees who worked for their management team. Relationship building usually is not about being the bad guy.

Second, almost without exception, the clients don't get as much practice disagreeing with people, and arguing with people, as their lawyers do. Practice doesn't always make you perfect, but it usually makes you better.

Being the bad guy didn't come naturally to me. I had to practice a lot before I got good at it. But eventually I got pretty good at it. An incident late in my in-house career provided some proof.

The Company had hired a software developer to develop some replacement software. The parties wrote a contract, unfortunately with no input from lawyers. The project began. And continued. And continued some more.

Like so many software development projects, this one suffered both maladies that often come with software development. First, the software developer, with a less than adequate understanding of the complexity of the project, over-promises, both as to timetable and as to cost. Second, the customer, in this case our Information Technology department, adds to the project's scope after the contract is signed, sometimes without even realizing that's what they're doing. They think the brief description of the project contained in the contract specifications covers what they're now asking for. It is a formula for disaster.

This particular project stretched on with no end in sight. Bills from the software firm piled up. Finally, the Company's management called a halt to the project. By that time, there were unpaid bills from the software developer that were over $1 million. And we faced the prospect of having to start from the beginning with a different software firm, with almost nothing usable from the work done to date.

I was the attorney for the Company. After some back and forth, the attorney for the software company and I agreed to meet with our clients at a mediation session. We picked a mediator. A senior executive from the Company went with me to the mediation meeting, along with several managers from our IT department.

The mediator suggested that each side make an opening statement to the other side's senior executive, which would be followed by the usual closeting of each side in separate rooms, with the mediator shuttling between the parties.

I made our Company's opening statement. I addressed myself to the senior executive of the software developer. I was very direct. I told him about the unpleasant future he and his company faced, detailing how I would show how his staff had lied to him, and to my clients, lies that included descriptions of progress they hadn't in fact made, and so-called successes on the project that weren't true. I described to him how substandard their work had been, and how much money we would collect from them in the lawsuit I was planning to file. Meanwhile, my client sat and didn't say a word, preserving his good guy status.

The mediation was a success. In the end, my client got to be the good guy, generously settling the matter for an amount that he had told me in advance was his goal, an amount that was substantially less than the software company was demanding. My client and the senior executive from the software development company held a brief but cordial meeting when the negotiations concluded.

As we were leaving the mediator's office, one of the IT managers from our Company said to me, "Steve, it happened that I was sitting right behind the senior executive from the software firm while you were talking to him. I can tell you that, facing toward you as you calmly read that guy the riot act, all I could think of was I hope I'm never on the opposite side from you. You are one tough cookie."

I have never thought of myself as a tough cookie. And even though I got good at it over time, I can't say it's fun to be the bad guy.

But it is fun to win. Make your choice.

CHAPTER 15

Work With People You Like

Lawyers sometimes take great pride in things that have little to do with liking their clients and being liked by them in return. We teach ourselves to value facts, objectivity, dispassionate rationality. Being a good lawyer sometimes means the very opposite of going along to get along.

I suppose it's possible to succeed as an in-house lawyer without having strong and positive relationships with your colleagues and clients. But I don't recommend trying it. The fact is that a lot of times your job is to say no. There's no getting around that. And in the long run, it is just easier to say no to people you like and who like you.

Here is another reason. Outside lawyers live for those phone calls and visits from clients. It's how they create billable hours. In-house lawyers have a somewhat different motivation. We want our clients to call and visit us often because if they do, the chances are greater that we can work on small problems and solve them before they become big problems. Think of it like preventive medicine.

In-house lawyers actually spend time thinking about how they can get their clients to check in with them before they (the clients) do the stupid things that are hard for lawyers to fix. I've been involved in a number of those Law Department idea sessions where we ask ourselves the question, how do we get the clients to come to us first? We come up with ideas and fill up flip charts. You can throw away the flip charts. At the end of most idea sessions that's what you do anyway. Because when you come right down to it, if the clients respect and like you, if getting your input is not like crawling over broken glass for them, they'll visit more often. For that you need the right kind of clients.

"It's the people."

Over and over again, the employees of International Harvester Company, and beginning in 1986, Navistar, consistently and universally have given that answer to the question, "What is the best thing about working at IH/Navistar?"

They faced that question often. The Company conducted its fair share of teambuilding training sessions and other activities where "What's the best thing about working here?" was the ice-breaker question. Management consultants came and went, and they all asked the Company employees whom they interviewed that same question. And no matter who asked it, the answer always was the same. It's the people. Long-time Company employees gave that answer so often, and heard their co-workers give that answer so often, that after a while, instead of simply saying "It's the people", Company employees expanded their answer, saying, "I know it sounds like a cliche, and that everybody says it, but it's really true. It's the people."

Why?

Were we incredibly talented, or lucky, in recruiting the very best people to work at the Company? People who knew how to work well with others, how to be good colleagues, whose definition of success did not include personal aggrandizement? People who knew how to achieve consensus without rancor?

Or did it have something to do with stress? Starting in the 1970s, and perhaps even earlier, the Company became a stressful place to work. There were strikes, there were corporate loans that couldn't be repaid, business reversals of all kinds, downsizings, layoffs. Was there something about the stress many of us felt as we tried to hold together the remnants of what had once been one of the biggest companies on the planet? Did that stress bring us closer together, like people huddled together against a storm? Did that stress create stronger camaraderie than existed at other companies? Were we so battered by the outside world, including our competitors, creditors, and others, that we bonded with each other that much more deeply?

Was it pride? Certainly the Company's employees were beneficiaries of proud traditions. When the odds makers and skeptics predicted the Company wouldn't last, was there something about the pride of being able to continue on despite those predictions? Do proud people like working with other proud people?

Was it simply because other things that might have topped the list of the best things about working at the Company weren't there? If the Company had been more profitable, with larger and more frequent bonuses and profit sharing payments, would we have been more likely to say that compensation was the best thing about the job?

With a strong presence in the middle of America, sometimes referred to as the Rust Belt, were we just enough alike to get along with each other well?

To be sure, not everyone thought that a company whose chief asset was its people, was a good thing. Some consultants, and some newly hired employees, especially the ones hired for management jobs, described the Company's corporate culture as "too nice". A new senior manager once said to me, "Everyone here is so polite, and so conflict avoidant. At my last job, if you looked at the clock and it was 9:00 am, and nobody in the company had yet screamed at you, or called you an incompetent idiot, you were having a good day."

Another of my colleagues told me he found the Company to be a very insular environment, hostile to outsiders. He joined Navistar in a senior manager role. Several years after he started, he explained his view. "Navistar's culture is not conducive to new hires, especially more senior employees like me. New employees here are treated with what seems like politeness. But in reality, a new Navistar employee is treated like an infection, and all of the long-time employees are like white blood cells that work to repel the outsider."

Maybe there was truth in what he said. But consider this. That manager continued to work for the Company for another 15 years. If we were antibodies, we clearly weren't very good at it, at least not in his case.

I worked for International Harvester, and then Navistar, for over 35 years, from 1981 to 2017. I worked with some people who were scheming corporate politicians. But not many. Some of my co-workers were prima donnas. But they were few in number. And I encountered a few people who hated their job and hated the Company. But if you looked at those people more closely, often you found that they hated a lot of things outside the Company as well. I always suspected that they would have hated any employer.

On the whole, through crises and upheavals, and big and little changes, I found myself agreeing with everyone who ever said that the best thing about the Company was its people.

Almost without exception, the people with whom I worked, inside the Law Department and everywhere else in the Company, were honest, hard-working people. They were good to each other. They supported each other.

In the late 1990s and through the first years of the following decade, many Navistar employees attended a training program whose emphasis was learning more about yourself and how you interacted with others. I took the course with my colleagues in the Law Department. After I completed the training course, I was asked to teach the course to other groups of Navistar employees. It made me wonder whether someone had decided I needed multiple refresher sessions, and making me a trainer was the best way to get that done.

One of the program's segments involved a discussion of what kind of leadership style you possess. There were four choices.

You might be a Controlling leader. Controllers were presented as decisive people who took charge, who made decisions and implemented them. Their weakness was that they sometimes ignored alternative points of view, and could seem cold and distant to their co-workers.

You might be an Analyzer. Analyzers were objective, thoughtful people who gathered information before moving forward. Their weaknesses included the fact that they tended to be overly formal, and too much in need of additional information before making a decision, sometimes to the point of "analysis paralysis".

You might be a Promoter. Promoters were people who thought up grand, entrepreneurial ideas and generated excitement about them among their co-workers. Promoters sometimes suffered from a tendency not to follow through and to fail to acknowledge any obstacles to their ideas.

Lastly there were the Supporters. Supporters were the people who worked to achieve consensus, who wanted everybody to be comfortable and happy with corporate decisions. Supporters were the people who cared a lot about their co-workers. They were called Supporters because they were supportive of others. Their weakness was a lack of decisiveness, and an aversion to decisions that were not fully supported by everyone.

In this particular training segment, the participants were exposed to, and discussed, the relative merits and downsides of each style. The point of the exercise was that no style was completely right or wrong, and that successful organizations in fact needed representatives of all four styles.

The end of the segment involved an exercise that identified the leadership style of each participant. Through self-analysis and feedback from co-workers, everyone identified himself or herself as being most like one of the styles. Controller, Analyzer, Promoter, Supporter. We put tape on the classroom floor to separate the training room into four parts. We placed large placards containing the names of the styles in each of the four quadrants. The participants rose and walked to stand in the quadrant representing their own particular style.

I led about 14 training sessions, each with at least 25 people in it. I did sessions for finance managers, accountants, IT staff, engineers, warehouse workers, and others. In every session the outcome of the exercise was amazingly similar. When the segment ended, a clear majority of people in the class were standing in the quadrant marked "Supporter".

Throughout my time at Navistar, the people I worked with showed great respect for their co-workers. Almost without exception, they did their best to take care of the people with whom they worked, in addition to tending to the Company's business. Navistar's managers did their best, both for the Company and for its people. They treated each other with respect. I liked them.

By the way, in the interest of full disclosure I should let you know that everyone who rated my leadership style labelled me a Controller. Not once did someone put me in the Supporter category.

So it's possible that I liked my Supporter co-workers because it was easy for a Controller like me to push them around.

I don't think that's true. But even if it is, I still liked them.

CHAPTER 16

Always Tell The Truth –
It Makes Everything Easier

"Always tell the truth" seems like a no-brainer rule. After all, lawyers are taught in law school to tell the truth. Tell the truth to the client. Tell the truth to others. The professional rules of conduct that govern our behavior address truthfulness. In Illinois, Rule 4.1 of the Professional Rules of Conduct reads:

"RULE 4.1: TRUTHFULNESS IN STATEMENTS TO OTHERS. In the course of representing a client a lawyer shall not knowingly:

(a) make a false statement of material fact or law to a third person…"

Rule 4.1 seems to offer exceptions. I am not an expert on ethics rules, but my reading of the rule suggests that it's not a violation to lie if you are not "in the course of representing a client". It is also not a violation if the lie you tell is not a "material fact".

My rule for in-house lawyers' success is broader.

First, take as a given that you are always "in the course of representing a client." Because even when you are sitting in the auditorium as just one more member of the audience in those all-employee meetings, or when you attend that software training class with co-workers from outside your department, no matter where you are, to the clients, you are the lawyer. In their minds, your presence alongside them means you are in the course of representing them.

Second, don't depend on whether your false statement is of a *"material"* fact. Clients may have trouble telling the difference.

Perhaps most importantly, recognize that as an in-house lawyer, your reputation within the corporation must include being honest and truthful all the time. In private practice, reputations can develop over time as you move from one client representation to another. In private practice, some client contacts can be characterized as transactions as opposed to relationships, but for an in-house lawyer, that's not the case. Inside a corporation, where you have the same client for as long as you remain on the payroll, your reputation becomes a permanent part of your "personal brand", beginning on your first day on the job.

In addition to these reasons, I believe strongly in in-house lawyer truthfulness for a reason that goes beyond morality and legal ethics. In the final analysis, the biggest benefit of consistently telling the truth is that it makes your job easier, including making it easier to win. The truth makes winning easier. I witnessed an example early in my career with the Company.

International Harvester's plant in Louisville, Kentucky was the scene of a large number of arbitrations. Partly this was a result of the fact that there were at least nine different bargaining units in the plant, represented by nine different unions. That's a lot of unions under one roof.

Clashes between unions were inevitable. I once represented the Company at an arbitration hearing where the issue was who got to flip a switch on the side of a cutting machine to add oil to the machine. Was it the machinist, who was represented by one union, or the oiler, who was represented by another union? I am not making this up. It was union vs. union with me in the middle.

One time I went to the Louisville plant for an arbitration hearing. I don't recall which union was the grievant. But on this occasion, it was just union versus management. The grievance had to do with numerically controlled cutting machines. In the Louisville plant there were machines that could cut metals into various shapes and sizes. The machine's operator would do measurements of the desired metal configuration, and then the operator would set mechanical controls on the cutting machine so that it would cut straight lines, turn left or right, make arcs, etc.

But then management bought some software that allowed a computer programmer to create a program that would "instruct" the machine as to the cutting route it should follow. The union argued that the machine operator, who was represented by the union, should do the computer programming that had replaced the old system of mechanical controls, the functions of which formerly had been done by the machine operator. Management argued that the computer programmer, who was not a union member, should do the programming.

At one of the grievance meetings leading up to the arbitration, our Labor Relations manager had told the union representatives that, among other reasons, the work couldn't be done by the unionized machine operator because computer programming required a college degree, and the machine operator didn't have one. I'm sure the Labor Relations manager thought that was a helpful thing to argue. But it struck a nerve with the union. The suggestion that their constituents were not educated enough to do the job just infuriated them. To them, arguing that a college degree was required was tantamount to management telling them they were too dumb to do the work.

Worse, it wasn't true. Some tasks might require a college degree but this wasn't one of them. The Labor Relations manager simply had made a mistake. Our formal response to the union didn't even mention academic credentials.

On the day before the arbitration hearing, I met with the witnesses from management who were going to testify at the hearing. It gave me a chance to learn more about the grievance. I talked with the computer programmer. He had a college degree. He wrote the program that controlled the cutting machine. I asked the programmer, who was not a union member, his opinion of whether the programming work required a college degree. He said no.

The next day the programmer sat in the witness chair. The attorney for the union cross-examined him. The attorney handed him a magazine article on how to program numerically controlled machines. The attorney asked him to read a particular sentence from the article. The programmer read aloud, "Programming work associated with numerically controlled machines requires a high school education."

The union's lawyer asked the programmer, "Do you agree with that statement?"

The programmer replied, "No, I do not."

I watched the union's lawyer. I could tell what he was thinking by the expression on his face. He was certain the programmer was going to say that a college degree was a requirement. His next move was going to be to call the Labor Relations manager, the person who'd floated the "college degree" defense, to the witness stand, where he would seek to embarrass him by making him read the same statement from the same magazine article.

Confident of his strategy, the union lawyer asked his next question.

"So if you don't agree that the requirement is a high school degree, then what level of education do you believe is required to do this work?"

With just the faintest smile on his face, the programmer replied, "I think about all you'd need is an 8th grade education. It's just not that hard."

I can't prove to you that the programmer's level of candor made everything else management said at the arbitration hearing that much more credible in the eyes of the arbitrator. The only proof I can offer is that we won the case.

In the 2000s, when I was General Counsel, Navistar went through a lengthy and significant restatement of its financial statements. Many previous accounting entries, going back several years, were incorrect. The Company's shareholders had to be told that they could not rely on our previous financial reports. The Audit Committee hired independent outside lawyers to investigate the Company's management. Those outside lawyers interviewed members of management to determine whether anyone had engaged in misconduct. The Securities and

Exchange Commission opened an investigation into the Company's accounting practices. The Company hired a consulting firm to help with the work of correcting the inaccurate accounting results.

All of the outsiders, whether lawyers, government investigators or consultants, looked at the rest of us with skepticism and even suspicion.

It was a tense time.

Six months after the restatement process began, the accountants, and the outside lawyers, and the outside consultants, still were not finished with their work.

One morning there was a meeting in my office. I don't remember everyone who was there, but I do recall that they included a senior member of the consulting firm. The meeting was about an accounting issue that was under review. One of the meeting participants, an accountant from one of the Company's divisions, remarked that the issue could be worse than previously thought. I don't recall his exact words, but he said something like, "This could be a much bigger hit to income than our current estimate. And it could affect more years' results than just the one we've been focusing on."

I also don't recall exactly what I said, but I do recall replying to him, saying something like, "Well, whatever it is, it is. If it's a big number, it's a big number. The only thing that's important is that it's right." To me, it wasn't a major pronouncement, just a simple statement of fact. I knew the accountant who was concerned about the issue. I had worked with him for years. I knew that he was a person of integrity. I knew he would agree that our goal was to get to the correct number. And he did agree. Everyone agreed. The meeting ended. Everyone left my office.

About two minutes later, the consultant who had been in the meeting reappeared at my office door. I thought maybe he'd left something behind. But he surprised me by saying, "Steve, I'm glad to find out that I can trust you."

I'm glad to find out that I can trust you.

People in corporate life sometimes refer to such times as "aha moments". That consultant's statement produced just such a moment for me. I had worked with him for almost six months. I had been honest and truthful in my interactions with him throughout that time.

But six months is not the same as six years, or even longer, which is how long most of my clients had known me. They knew I told the truth. He wasn't sure. That consultant needed to hear me express my determination to be honest and truthful.

The benefit of that exchange was immediate. After that day, it was easier for me to work with that consultant. He told me things I needed to hear, confident that I would respond appropriately. He was more open and forthcoming about his findings as he reviewed our accounting. And because he trusted me, whenever I provided clarifications and explanations for some of what he found, he knew that what he was hearing was truth, not coverup. In a word, things became easier.

In a restatement, there is no way of winning. But handled the wrong way, there are ways to lose. We didn't lose.

After that exchange with the consultant, I redoubled my efforts to let people know that I was honest. I made sure that everyone outside the Company, as well as inside the Company, knew that I could be counted on for the truth. Whenever the occasion permitted, and especially when I was talking with people outside Navistar, I went out of my way to emphasize my determination that they would only hear the truth.

At the end of the restatement process, the Company's Board of Directors decided to appoint a Chief Ethics Officer.

They chose their General Counsel.

CHAPTER 17

Don't Be the Client –
Unless There's No Other Choice

My experience is that clients make the best clients. Lawyers as clients come in a pretty distant second.

I once was handling a very large, high profile lawsuit in a federal court in a medium size city several hours away from the Company's headquarters. I went to the trial every day to watch as the Company's outside counsel dueled with counsel for a large class of plaintiffs.

It occurred to someone back at headquarters that the trial might end without enough warning for someone from our Corporate Communications staff to be able to get to the courthouse to answer the expected media questions. That would mean that I, as the highest ranking Company representative on-site, would have to be the Company's spokesperson. It was decided by someone that I should receive media training. Just in case.

The Company hired a former TV investigative reporter to do the training. We did practice interviews. She taught me about eye contact, about using something called the bridge statement to get back to the points I wanted to make. We practiced what I should say if we won.

We practiced what I should say if we lost. She spent about three hours with me. When we were done, she asked me if she could be candid with me. I said sure.

She said, "Steve, you are better than when we started, but if I were you, I would do everything in my power to avoid ever being interviewed by someone in the media. You should let your clients do all the talking." The funny thing is that I had been thinking the exact same thing.

I learned that lesson well. I handled the closing of the sale of the Company's plant in Memphis, Tennessee. After the closing, the participants invited the TV reporters into the closing room. The Memphis mayor talked. Other politicians talked. The mayor and the other politicians answered questions from the reporters.

Someone then asked if anyone from International Harvester was present. The closing had been a last-minute thing and there was no client with me. I was the only Company representative at the closing. I raised my hand. The mayor said, "would you like to say something, sir"?

My reply? "No, thank you." I'm pretty sure that clip didn't make the 6 o'clock news.

Clients also are the people who testify at depositions and trials. Not lawyers. And there is a good reason for that. I will explain.

I am not sure, but I believe I may hold a record among in-house lawyers. I was deposed as a fact witness, or called to the witness stand at a trial or hearing, more than 15 times during my career as an in-house lawyer. I don't know the exact number. I lost count somewhere after the 15th time.

It's not that I wanted to be a witness. But too often during the Company's downsizing days, I worked with clients who got downsized out of the Company, leaving me as the only person from the team who still worked at the Company, the only person who knew anything about the subject of a particular dispute.

You would think that after being deposed and questioned so many times, I would have gotten better at it. And you would be wrong. I actually seemed to get worse.

In one of my first experiences, early in my career at International

Harvester, I testified in an administrative hearing. I can't remember why. I can only hope it wasn't my idea. But I can't be sure.

At my request, our outside counsel had prepared me just like he would a real client. I listened to the advice I myself had given to others. Listen to the question. Don't answer right away. Give your lawyer time to object. Listen to the objection. Only answer the question that's being asked. Don't volunteer additional information. Don't guess. Tell the truth.

I was ready.

The hearing was to determine whether International Harvester had good cause to terminate one of its dealers. At the hearing, our outside counsel called me to testify. I listened carefully, determined to follow his advice. He asked, "Can you tell us the reasons why the company terminated the dealer?"

My answer? "Yes."

That's it. "Yes." Determined not to volunteer, determined to answer only the question that was asked, I ludicrously chose to be super-literal and say that yes, I was able to provide that information. Our outside counsel looked at me, puzzled. And then it dawned on him. I could almost see it in his expression. "Oh, I get it. You're a lawyer." But what he actually said was, "Please tell the hearing officer those reasons."

And if you think I got better after additional practice, you would need to think again. One of my final depositions was in an employment termination case. I went through the same preparation session with our outside counsel. The opposing counsel, seated opposite me, questioned me for several hours. His tone was belligerent. He was seated next to his client, the plaintiff, our former employee. The opposing lawyer definitely was showing his client, and all of us, that he was a tough and combative questioner.

Finally, our outside counsel decided an objection was in order. He said, "Objection. You have been harassing my client all morning, and you are continuing to do it, and I want it to stop."

And of course the plaintiff's lawyer was in fact harassing me. He'd been doing it all morning. But by that time in my career I had been in countless encounters with tough, combative people. It comes with the job. It seemed like just another day to me.

The opposing lawyer said to me, "Mr. Covey, do you feel harassed?"

Give your lawyer time to object. Listen to the objection.

My answer? "No. I'm ok."

I ask you, would you want me as a client?

But believe it or not, those examples don't represent my worst performance as a client.

That story requires some background.

At one time, International Harvester Company was so vertically integrated that we owned our own steel mill. It was called Wisconsin Steel even though it was located in Chicago. Go figure. Not only did we own our own steel mill, we also owned the ore boats that brought the raw materials to the mill. We even owned our own coal mine that produced coal for the mill. The coal mine, called Benham Coal Company, was in southern Kentucky.

International Harvester Company sold the Wisconsin Steel Mill in the late 1970s. The steel mill had ceased operations by the early 1980s. Meanwhile, the Benham Coal Company, no longer a supplier to Wisconsin Steel, kept operating, selling coal to other customers.

In the mid-1980s, someone at the Company decided that we didn't need to own a coal mine anymore. I was on the team assigned to find a buyer.

I was a Chicago lawyer who knew nothing about coal mining. Nothing. But, I got on the plane with the other members of our small team and flew down to southern Kentucky.

The Benham Coal managers were very polite. They took us on a tour. They offered to let us board one of the flat cars that travelled into the mines, where, a mile or so from the entrance, the coal was being dug. As politely as I could, I declined. After all, the miners knew we were there to sell the company that employed them. It just didn't seem like a good idea to ride on a little car into a pitch-black coal mine where people who soon were likely going to be unemployed were waiting to greet me.

I remember one moment during the tour when the managers

showed us the coal washing equipment that had just been installed. It was near the entrance of the mine. The coal was running down a long conveyor belt inside a sluice that was filled with water. The managers were pleased with it.

But I was just dumbfounded. Why would you wash coal? I could see that the coal was dirty. After all, it had just been dug out of the ground. But why did it need to be cleaned?

I asked the Benham manager, "Why do you wash the coal? Isn't it clean enough to be sold as is?" The manager smiled, and in his soft Kentucky accent explained.

"We call it washing, but it's really a process to separate the coal from the rocks. As the material from the mine travels along the conveyor belt, the rocks sink. The coal floats. At the end of the line, we dump the rocks and what we're left with is all coal."

I thought then that I was lucky that the Benham Coal manager was such a polite person. I can only imagine what he thought about being represented by a lawyer who thought coal needed to be cleaned!

Eventually we found a buyer for the coal mine. In the meantime, the coal mine had shut down, and all of the mine employees had been terminated. That included the managers of Benham Coal who had served as the officers of the Benham Coal Company.

We were approaching the closing. The closing process required that an officer of the Benham Coal Company sign deeds and other closing documents. Only there were no Benham Coal Company officers left. And I didn't have a client at headquarters who knew anything about the deal. My only client for the transaction was a manager in the Treasury Department whose only interest was how quickly could we close and get the money.

I thought about trying to contact the former manager of the coal mine, who lived in southern Kentucky, and ask him to agree to be re-elected as a Vice President of Benham Coal. It's what I should have done. But I would have had to track him down, and then explain why we needed him to serve as an officer again, and then make some compensation deal with him. And it just seemed easier to skip all that by naming myself a Vice President of Benham Coal. After all, at least I knew what coal washing was!

I wrote a board of directors resolution naming me a Vice President of the Benham Coal Company. It's one of many seemingly small actions I took as an in-house lawyer that I wouldn't mind taking back.

It's not that I had any trouble at the closing. In fact, it was a nice change of pace to attend a closing where I didn't have to bother explaining the closing documents to the client who was signing them. I was the client. The deal closed, we got our money, and I probably congratulated myself on coming up with what lawyers sometimes call "an elegant solution".

But that wasn't the end of it.

Benham Coal Company had leased some of its land to a strip-mining company. In preparation for closing, the lease had been terminated. The unhappy strip miners sued Benham Coal Company. They demanded a jury trial in the small Kentucky town where Benham had operated.

I remember going to the town of Benham, Kentucky to attend the trial. At the entrance to the courthouse, there was a large plaque that described in detail how "Yankee troops" had burned the original courthouse during the U.S. Civil War. Yankee troops. I am not making that up.

And here was I, the lawyer from up north in Chicago, sitting at the counsel's table for the trial, acting as the corporate representative for Benham Coal Company, looking at a jury whose friends and neighbors had lost their jobs when the Benham Coal mine shut down.

I thought my only task would be to sit up straight, look interested, and observe the proceedings. You know. Be the client. I was going to keep a low profile.

Keeping a low profile went out the window when the attorney for the strip-miners announced that I was his first witness! I took the witness stand and began answering his questions.

"Mr. Covey, what is your position with the Benham Coal Company?"

I wanted to answer, "Well, I'm a Vice President. But not really. I just needed a client to sign some papers and I picked me". But I knew that would only sound stupid. So I just said, "I am the company's Vice President."

"And is your office here in Kentucky?"

"No."

"Where is it?"

"Chicago."

"And where do you live?"

"Chicago."

"Benham Coal is a subsidiary of the International Harvester Company, is that correct?"

"Yes."

"And where are the headquarters of International Harvester Company?"

"Chicago."

I don't remember the rest of his questions but I think they required me to say "Chicago" another four or five times in the first five minutes of my testimony. It began to seem almost funny to me. I was tempted to ask whether he thought the jurors had gotten it by now or should I just confess that I was a Yankee.

He never asked a single question about coal washing.

As my testimony ended, I wanted to say to the jurors, "I'm really sorry about burning down your courthouse during the Civil War." But I decided I was probably the only one who would see the humor in that. And besides, it probably would have been stricken from the record anyway.

Every so often, you have no choice and you have to assume the role of client. But if you do have a choice, I strongly recommend that you choose to be the lawyer and let the client be the client.

Especially if you are a Yankee.

CHAPTER 18

Be Creative Wisely – And as Seldom as Possible

Creativity is a very useful attribute, even for lawyers. Class action lawsuits, product liability torts, the poison pill. At one time they didn't exist. It took creative lawyers to dream them up and turn them into useful legal tools.

But for in-house lawyers, the emphasis is more on the simple, the already tested and confirmed, the solutions that everyone knows will work.

I worked with a very talented lawyer at International Harvester who also was very creative, sometimes too creative. He once lost an arbitration hearing against one of our unions. He was certain that the arbitrator had exceeded his authority and somehow violated the U.S. Constitution in the process. My colleague ended up presenting a unique and creative constitutional argument to a federal appellate court. I forget the details of his argument, but I remember it cost the Company a lot of money to take it through the appeals process. The appellate court ruled against him. He appealed to the U.S. Supreme Court. They denied his certiorari petition. Unanimously.

My colleague had temporarily forgotten that we were in the business of making trucks and farm equipment, not in the business of coming up with creative legal arguments in order to set new legal precedents.

Sometimes, though, circumstances force you to exercise some creativity. And you have to be ready when that times comes.

I did the legal work for the sale of one of our Company's closed manufacturing plants. After searching for commercial buyers for a while, we decided to sell the plant to the city in which it was located. The purchase price was one dollar. The city's plan was to lease the plant to small businesses in an incubator type arrangement, with the hope that the city could thereby create new jobs for its residents.

Everyone liked the plan, including the governor of the state, who sent a staff member to meet with me the day before the closing. The governor's aide told me the governor was going to fly in to attend the closing. I said that would be great. Our CEO also was going to attend the closing. So was the mayor of the city. We were going to do the closing in a conference room at the plant and then there would be a press conference on the plant floor, which would present a great photo opportunity. Everyone would be a winner.

But then the governor's aide threw me a curve. "Steve," he said, "the governor wants to be a part of the closing. He needs something to sign in front of the cameras."

"There's nothing for the governor to sign," I replied. "The state is not a party to the contract. The only parties are the seller, that's my company, and the buyer, that's the city. Besides, a real estate closing like this is a complicated process that doesn't fit well with a media event."

The aide smiled broadly at me and said, "You look like a creative guy, Steve. I'm sure you'll think of something."

I gave it some thought. That evening I wrote a document entitled "Closing Memo". It contained one short paragraph, which read, "We, the undersigned, hereby state that we were present this day for the closing." I inserted two signature lines, one for the mayor, and one for the CEO. Then I added a third line that read, "The undersigned witnessed the above signatures." That one was for the governor.

I made six copies of the Closing Memo. The next morning, at 7:30 am, I met with the city attorney, the city manager, the representative from the title company, and our real estate manager. We signed and exchanged closing documents. There were a lot of them. Finally, we were done, just in time for the 9:00 am press conference.

Our CEO, the city's mayor, and the state's governor were seated at a table facing the cameras. I took the six Closing Memos from my briefcase and placed two copies in front of each signer. The cameras were turned on. The three men took turns signing documents and passing them to each other, all the while smiling for the cameras and chatting amiably with each other. The signing took about two minutes. The documents were of course meaningless. But I collected them from the table anyway.

Here is the amusing part. As I looked at the six documents, I discovered that on three of them, the signers had signed on the wrong signature lines. The governor had signed for the mayor, our CEO had signed for the governor, and the mayor had signed on the signature line for the CEO. On two of the documents, there was at least one signature missing. And the sixth copy had no signatures at all. I thought for a moment about what it would have been like if I had tried to conduct the real closing at the press conference. The thought made me cringe.

Later that day, I watched the local news report on television. As the reporter talked, the pictures showed the CEO, the mayor and the governor signing my Closing Memos. I wondered whether there were any real estate lawyers watching the TV news and asking themselves how you could close a complicated deal like that with so few pieces of paper.

Some years after that real estate closing, I became the Company's Corporate Secretary. In addition to the responsibility for setting agendas and writing minutes of meetings of the Board of Directors, I attended the Company's shareholder meetings.

We held our shareholder meetings in a large auditorium in Chicago. Our shareholder meetings in recent years had featured picketers from one of our closed locations. They were protesting our handling of their employee benefits. As a result, we followed a tight script for our shareholder meetings to minimize the opportunities for disruptions. There never were any disruptions, but better to be safe, as the saying goes.

Usually, proposals at a shareholder meeting required only a majority of the shares either present at the meeting in person, or by proxy, to vote in favor of them. But at this particular shareholder meeting, we were presenting an extremely serious proposal that required a majority of all the outstanding shares for approval. My staff had worked hard to get the maximum number of shareholders to vote. Most shareholders vote in advance of the meeting. By the day of the meeting, well over 80% of the total number of outstanding shares had been cast in favor of the proposal, far more than we needed. Approval of the proposal was a foregone conclusion. Not many people attended our shareholder meetings in person, and collectively they usually represented less than 1/100 of 1% of the outstanding shares.

At the meeting, our CEO followed the script. He stood up and described the proposal. He asked if anyone had any questions. A few people did. The CEO answered them. Then he consulted his script and continued, "If you sent us your proxy, you don't have to vote again unless you want to change your vote. If you didn't send us your proxy, you can vote your shares using the card we gave you when you entered the meeting. Simply fill it in and raise your hand. One of the ushers will then take your ballot to our election judges, who are offstage."

Nobody had ever voted in person. Most of the people who attended our shareholder meetings were Company retirees who had come to renew old acquaintances and get a free donut.

The CEO paused, just like the script told him to do. And wouldn't you know it, a guy in the front row raised his hand. He wanted to vote in person. An usher went to him and took his ballot. She started walking up the aisle to the rear of the auditorium. Not knowing what else to do, the CEO looked down at his script and read the next part, "Steve, would you please present the report of the election judges."

I stood up and went to the microphone. I had the judge's tally, which showed overwhelming support for the proposal. I looked down at my script, which called for me to say, "Mr. Chairman, the proposal has been approved by a majority of the outstanding shares of the Company."

I looked at the shareholder in the first row who had just voted. I had met that man. He owned about 200 shares. Out of about 200 million. No matter which way he had voted, the outcome was going to be the same. I thought about saying something to that effect, but I couldn't think of how to say it without embarrassing the shareholder. While these thoughts were going through my head, the usher was still walking up the aisle with his ballot. How would it look if I announced the results of the voting before she even left the auditorium?

On the other hand, if I waited until the usher delivered the man's vote to the judges, and waited for them to print out a new vote tally and bring it to me, it would mean a delay of 10-15 minutes. Nobody wanted to wait that long. Not even the guy with the 200 shares. And when it was all done, I would be using the exact same script that I was holding in my hand, informing the shareholders that the measure had been approved.

I made my decision. Ignoring the script, I said, "Mr. Chairman, I have a preliminary report from the judges, but they have not yet counted the vote of the shareholder in the first row who voted in person. I will be right back."

And I walked off the stage.

I give the CEO credit. He didn't look at me like I was an idiot. He didn't say anything. He sat on the stage, patiently waiting for me to return. In the meantime, I left the stage and stood behind the stage curtain. I slowly counted to ten. And then I walked back out, went to the microphone, and said, "Mr. Chairman, the proposal has been approved by a majority of the outstanding shares of the Company."

Many years later I was sitting in the chambers of a federal judge. I was there for a settlement conference. It was not going well. The judge was doing his best to bring the parties together but the only one doing any compromising was me. Finally I had had enough. But the judge made one more try to see if I would increase my offer yet again. He urged me and the other Company representatives to take some time and think about making yet another offer. He said he would leave the room. He told us to think about our position, take all the time we needed to decide whether to come up with a new offer, and then call him when we were ready with our answer.

The judge had asked us to take some time to think about it. I did. It's just that I was done thinking about five seconds after the judge left the room.

But I had learned enough about federal judges to know that it's important not to annoy them if you can possibly avoid it. I turned to our outside counsel and said, "Have I ever told you the story of the time someone voted in person at one of our shareholder meetings?" Looking puzzled, the outside counsel said no. I proceeded to tell him the story, complete with the part about my counting to ten and then coming back on stage. Then I said, "So here is what I want you to do. Count to ten and then go get the judge and as politely as you can, tell him our last offer was our last offer."

Creativity is a useful tool in the right circumstances for an in-house lawyer. The challenge with creativity is that it must always reflect the underlying truth. My assembly plant sale had in fact closed before my ceremonial Closing Memo was signed. And that shareholder proposal had in fact been approved, with or without those 200 votes. That's why my rule is to be creative wisely. And as seldom as possible.

CHAPTER 19

If Your Client Asks You to
Go With Them – Go

Outside lawyers love to be asked to travel with their clients. It's not that they like business trips any more than do the in-house lawyers. But they know it builds relationships. During the inevitable downtime at airports, the get to have informal chats with their client, which gives them an opportunity to talk about their value, and their law firm's value, to the client's business. Plus, they generally get to bill by the hour, and traveling takes up a lot of hours. And, perhaps most importantly, the entire trip only requires filling out one time slip. Win, win, win, win.

But for in-house lawyers, it is a different story. We have all the time we need to build relationships with the client. Whenever I met with candidates to join our Law Department, if they asked me what was different about practicing law inside a corporation, I always talked about the ubiquitousness of the client. If you went to the cafeteria, the client was at the next table. In the parking lot, the client was in the next parking space. When you stood washing your hands in the bathroom, the client was standing at the sink next to you. Wherever you went, there was the client. That's a lot of relationshiping.

With all of that closeness, every day brings another opportunity to show the client how valuable we are. So you don't need that downtime at airports to sell yourself. And anyway, even if they don't see how valuable we are, they're stuck with us. Just like we're stuck with them.

And we don't fill out time slips. All lawyers hate filling out time slips. I have known in-house lawyers who said that their chief motivation for going in-house was that they would never have to fill out time slips again. They were only half joking. After I became General Counsel, whenever I wanted to wake up the lawyers at my staff meeting, I would casually suggest that maybe we should start filling out time slips so that we could measure which business groups used us the most. It always worked. Suddenly the energy level in the room went way up, as first one lawyer, then another, would start listing all the reasons why it was a terrible idea. It was kind of cruel of me to do that, but I have to admit it also was kind of fun.

So why should you say yes whenever the client asks you to go with them?

Well, this is one of those rules for in-house lawyers that, if you have to ask why, you probably shouldn't be practicing law in a corporate law department. But perhaps this story will help you.

I had been working at International Harvester, and then Navistar, for 20 years. I had moved on from being the finance and securities lawyer to the job of General Counsel of the Company's finance subsidiary, Navistar Financial Corporation. I was comfortable. I liked my co-workers.

Finance companies can seem very complicated to an outsider. For the in-house lawyers, the legal work involved a lot of Uniform Commercial Code, bankruptcy law, and a working knowledge of asset backed securitizations. That's how we raised the money we loaned out. But in the end, it was a pretty simple business. We loaned money to our customers. And if they didn't repay us, we repossessed their trucks.

I travelled a little but not much. And never very far. And then one

December morning I got a call from a former client in the Company's Engine Division.

"Hi, Steve," he said. "It's been a while. How are things going?"

"Fine," I replied. "How are things in Engine?"

"Just great. In fact, do you remember that deal we did together four years ago to buy 50% of that engine company in Brazil? And you included in the contract an option for us to acquire the other 50%? Well, we want to exercise that option, and we'd like you to go to Brazil with us to work on the deal."

I hesitated. "Well, I work in another Company division now. I would have to ask my boss if it's ok."

"He'll say yes. This is a big deal."

I hesitated some more. "And what about the Engine Division's General Counsel? Won't she mind?"

"She'll be happy for you to do it. It lightens her workload. And besides, you know the deal, and we worked well together last time."

I was running out of excuses fast.

I was hesitating because I had never seemed to get the hang of travelling to Brazil. I liked the country. And I liked the people. I also liked the clients with whom I travelled. But it was a very long flight from Chicago. And even though I travelled in business class, and sometimes in first class, the trip was tiring, and our corporate style of working was always to get right off the plane and go straight into the first meeting, challenging my powers of concentration.

Then there was the language. On one of my first trips to Brazil I flew alone. The clients were already there. My plane landed in Sao Paulo and I made my connection for the flight from Sao Paulo to Porto Alegre. For that flight, I was on a Brazilian airline. All of the announcements were in Portuguese. I took four years of high school Spanish. And Portuguese and Spanish share some words. But not as many as you'd think. So when the drink cart came to my row, and the young flight attendant said something to me in Portuguese, I decided that I would not admit that I didn't know the language. I thought I should have no trouble ordering coffee. I replied, "Café negro, por favor." Black coffee, please. That should do it. The flight attendant, who was dark skinned, noticeably stiffened, but poured out a cup of coffee and wordlessly handed it to me.

At dinner that evening, I was talking with one of the Brazilian managers, and I told the story to him. I asked him,

"Did I say something that was wrong?"

"Steve, you used a word that doesn't mean the same thing in Spanish that it means in Portuguese."

"Which word?"

"Negro. In Spanish, negro means black. In Mexico City I'm sure you had no trouble getting black coffee. But in Portuguese, negro is not such a good word. You have a word in America that is the equivalent. I think you call it the N word."

"Oh no! You mean he thought I was calling him the N word?"

"Perhaps not," my colleague said diplomatically. "But from now on, you should order 'café preto'." He smiled. "Or just say 'Coke'."

Then there was the time I took my one and only cab ride alone in Brazil. My clients and I were meeting with our local counsel at his office in Sao Paulo. The meeting lasted all day. It was time for dinner. My clients wanted to go back to our hotel. But the local counsel and I had some more work to do, work that didn't require the clients' presence. I insisted that they not wait. I would finish up and then join them later for dinner.

They left. An hour later, the local counsel and I were finished. He ordered a taxi for me. He rode down in the elevator with me. He waited with me for the taxi to pull up in front of the office building. I thanked him and started to walk outside.

"Wait," he said. "I will walk you to the car."

Jokingly, I replied, "I think I know the way to the curb."

"Yes, but you don't know Sao Paulo. It can be a very dangerous place, especially after dark. Also, I will tell the driver the name and address of your hotel so there will be no mistakes."

We walked to the taxi. I got into the back seat. My Brazilian colleague spoke to the driver in Portuguese. The driver nodded.

The taxi ride from the hotel to our local counsel's office had taken about 10 minutes earlier that day, when the traffic had been heavier.

So it seemed a little odd to me when 15 minutes passed and we still hadn't arrived at the hotel. I looked out the taxi window. Nothing looked familiar. I told myself that there was no reason for anything to look familiar. I told myself that same thing for another 10 minutes. Then we turned into a very dark, and very deserted looking, side street. The driver seemed to be looking from side to side.

I had visions of being robbed. Or worse. I worked to remain calm. I still didn't know any Portuguese. I tried my Spanish. At least I wasn't ordering black coffee.

"Donde esta el hotel"?

The driver didn't reply. Instead, he turned down another dark side street.

I switched to English and tried again. "Where is the hotel?"

Again, no reply.

Another ten minutes went by. I was still alive. I still had my wallet. And then, finally, the hotel was in sight. When the driver pulled up to the front door, I could not have been more relieved. As I reached for my wallet, the driver waved the hotel doorman over. He said something in Portuguese.

The doorman said to me, "Your driver wants to apologize because he got lost. He is very embarrassed. He doesn't want you to pay anything."

What I said was, "Please tell him there is no need for apologies. These things happen. I am happy to pay."

What I wanted to say was, "Please tell him that 10 minutes ago I was in fear for my life. The exorbitant fare showing on the meter is nothing compared to what I thought this trip was going to cost."

Now it was several years later. As all of this went through my mind, my Engine Division client waited for my answer.

"Sure," I said. "I'd be happy to go with you."

I would like to say that I was following my own rule about going with the client whenever they asked, but I suspect that a small part of my decision was that it was freezing cold that December in Chicago, and Brazil was in the middle of its summer.

The trip lasted almost a week. And inevitably there was a second trip several weeks later for the closing. The night before the closing, there was a dinner. The head of Navistar's Engine Division had flown down for the closing. He hosted the dinner. As part of his after-dinner talk, he singled me out and thanked me for doing the legal work on the deal. The next day, when he offered a toast at lunch immediately after the closing, he recognized me again. "I can't thank Steve enough for helping us on this deal. You know, he works at the finance company now, which is a completely separate division, and he didn't have to do this. I am very grateful that he came all the way to Brazil to finish what he helped us start four years ago."

Three years later, he moved from running the Engine Division to running the whole company as its CEO.

Six months after that, he chose me to be the Company's next General Counsel.

I am sure it was because of my wealth of experience and my superior legal skills. Pretty sure, anyway.

But if your client asks you to go with them – go. You never know.

BONUS SECTION

How to Be a Successful General Counsel

The Three Reasons You Should Read this Section

Y ou probably don't need reasons to read this bonus section. For example, if you have benefitted from reading the previous chapters, you'll continue reading, even if you have no aspirations to be a General Counsel. What do you have to lose?

If you have not benefitted from reading the previous chapters, you are likely confident enough, or perhaps arrogant enough, to have told yourself, as you read chapter after chapter, "That's not helpful. I already knew that." If you are that person, the likelihood is you will turn the page and continue reading so that you can have the satisfaction, chapter by chapter, of telling yourself, "I already knew that, too."

Either way, here are the three reasons you should read this section.

1. **I am not the only game in town, but it's pretty close.**

I did some research and could not find many books on how to be a successful General Counsel. So what follows likely will be among the best advice you will get, because there is so little advice available to you. One cautionary note. I am not an exceptional researcher. Before deciding that I have written one of the few, if not the only, how-to manual on being a successful General Counsel, the only research I did was to complete a Google search using the search phrase "Books on how to be a successful General Counsel". If it turns out that I picked the wrong search term, and that in fact there are lots of instructional guides out there for being a successful General Counsel, please accept my apologies.

2. **Even if I'm not the only game in town, you should pay attention to me because I made a Top 100 list.**

Once during my tenure as General Counsel, I picked up a magazine for in-house lawyers. I was attracted to an article that contained a list of the 100 most highly compensated General Counsels at American public companies. As I browsed through the list, I discovered my name. I think I was somewhere around 68th. Only 67 GCs made more money than I did. Candidly, I don't think that my compensation is of any particular importance in determining whether I can offer useful advice on how to be a successful General Counsel. But maybe you think so. If you do, then until one of the top 67 General Counsels writes a book, I am your best bet.

3. **If you're reading this, it probably means you've read all of the chapters that preceded it. So why not just finish the whole book?**

CHAPTER 20

Choose the Right Outside Counsel

Outside counsel are very important people. You need them. They offer expertise and depth. The nature of their work usually means that they have faced hundreds of times the situation that you may be facing for the first time.

When it comes to litigation, they tend to spend their time in deposition rooms and courtrooms. The rooms where you tend to spend more of your time are your company's conference rooms. Which makes outside counsel better candidates to handle your lawsuits for you.

Outside counsel also do things that you frankly just don't have time to do. Early in my in-house career, a lawyer representing someone who had a grievance against the Company kept calling and calling me. I was very busy. He was very persistent. Finally on one of his calls, he said, "Mr. Covey, if you continue to be unwilling to resolve this matter, I am going to file suit against International Harvester Company." I replied, "Gee, I wish you would. Because then I could hire outside counsel and I wouldn't have to talk to you anymore." As an aside, I am not recommending this approach as a tactic in dealing with opposing counsel. Although that lawyer didn't file a lawsuit and never called me again. Probably just a coincidence.

At International Harvester Company, and at Navistar, our unwritten policy was that the in-house lawyer who was assigned a particular matter had the freedom to choose who to hire in situations where we needed the help of outside counsel. Even during the period of time in the 1980s when our General Counsel was a senior partner at one of our outside law firms, we never were pressured to use his firm in making our outside counsel selections.

That said, your situation might be different. Maybe in your law department, the outside counsel decisions are made by the General Counsel. But even if that is not the case, and you follow the Navistar model of letting the individual lawyers in your department make the outside counsel choices, in the very biggest cases you handle, it's likely that you will at least put a thumb on the scale for the outside counsel you want. And when you are the General Counsel, one thumb is usually all it takes to get your way. You can ask my staff.

Sadly, there is no perfect system for picking outside counsel. I thought about not even trying to write this chapter. But it's such a critical part of the job that I decided to offer to you what I learned, for whatever help it may be.

A perfect system would be based on a wealth of data that would tell you, particular matter by particular matter, which firm, and more specifically, which attorney in which firm, has the best ability to produce the best outcome for the best price. The challenge in achieving that perfection is obvious. It reminds me of a story told by Jack Brickhouse, the former announcer for Chicago Cubs baseball games. He told the story of some baseball legend, I forget who, who said, "There is no such thing as a perfect pitch. Because in order for a pitch to be perfect, it would have to be in the strike zone. And if it's in the strike zone, it can be hit. And if it can be hit, it's not perfect."

Most in-house lawyers are under pressure to hire the least expensive counsel who can do the work. I bargain shopped for outside counsel once solely based on the hourly rates of my outside counsel. I ended up with a million dollar loss in a case where the plaintiff who was suing

Navistar originally had demanded $300,000. The attorneys' fees I paid to our outside counsel were about $200,000 less than they would have been if I had hired a pricier law firm. You can do the math.

But when hiring outside counsel from the big, expensive firms, consideration has to be given to whether you are bringing in bigger guns than you need. Once I hired a lawyer who worked at a large law firm, a very expensive law firm. The plaintiff who was suing Navistar was asking for $100,000. The outside counsel won the case, including on appeal. The plaintiff collected nothing. The outside counsel's total fee: $375,000.

Generally you get great expertise at the biggest law firms. Plus you get the benefit of the firm's name recognition in front of the judge, which is not a bad thing. But before throwing up your hands and hiring the biggest, most expensive law firm in town for your biggest cases, consider this. On two occasions when I did just that, I was disappointed. Two separate, and very large, law firms. Two separate, and very large, lawsuits, the kind that, if you are a public company, get prominently mentioned in your SEC filings.

In the first matter, the law firm I hired advised me that we should settle the case for between $35 million and $40 million. I didn't take the advice. The case settled for just under $3 million.

In the second matter, the advice from yet another very large and well respected firm was that we should settle the case for $40 million to $50 million. I didn't take that advice either. That case settled for zero dollars and some non-monetary consideration.

Fairness requires that I note that the successful settlements in both cases were greatly aided by the work done by those big law firms leading up to the settlement negotiations. But still.

Don't misunderstand me. Sometimes a very large firm with a national reputation is exactly what you need. As one General Counsel once told me, "If you win the big cases, you can use any firm. But if you lose the big cases, you'd better have used a law firm that your board of directors has heard of."

While you wait for that perfect system to tell you who to hire, here are some tips I learned.

- **Whenever possible, hire the lawyer, not the firm.** The best outside counsel I ever knew started his career at a very large law firm. He produced excellent results for the Company whenever we hired him. He ended up leaving that large firm to start a small firm with a group of other lawyers. The Company continued to hire him. He continued to produce excellent results. Several years later his small firm merged with a very large firm. The Company continued to hire him, and he continued to produce excellent results. Only from then on he charged a lot more. Near the end of his career he started his own firm. By that time I had learned that it didn't matter which firm he worked for. The only thing that mattered was him.

- **In litigation, it's great to have a good trial lawyer, but even greater to have a lawyer who knows how to win before trial.** That best outside counsel, the one I mentioned in the immediately preceding tip was, I'm pretty sure, an excellent trial lawyer. I can't be 100% sure because he never went to trial for the Company. He never needed to. I never saw him make a closing argument. I never even saw him make an opening argument. His skill was in winning motions to dismiss and summary judgments. He had a unique ability to think ahead, to anticipate his opponent's next move, and the one after that. He was a chess player among checkers players. Successful outcomes in litigation can come at any phase of the process. Sometimes the wins come sooner, sometimes later. My experience was that sooner was better.

- **Make sure the outside counsel you hire is the outside counsel you get.** I had more than one experience of hiring a senior partner at a law firm and then never talking to him or her again. There's nothing per se wrong with using talented junior partners and associates. In some cases you actually will get a better result. And of course, you will save money along the way. The kids cost less. But consistent with the advice that you should hire the lawyer, not the firm, my advice is that you find out up front whether the lawyer you hire plans to be personally involved in your matter on a day to day basis. And if not, either continue shopping before choosing your outside counsel, or interview the junior lawyers who will be handling your case and make your decision based on your perceptions of them.

- **Hire an outside counsel who has the same objectives you have.** I once handled a lawsuit that involved a piece of innovative technology developed by one of our employees. The technology was embedded in a critical component of a critical product produced by Navistar. We got sued. The plaintiff alleged (1) that the plaintiff, not our employee, had invented the technology, (2) that our patent was invalid, and (3) that the plaintiff, not us, had the exclusive right to use the technology. I still remember the phone call from our outside counsel when the trial ended. "I have good news," he said, excitement in his voice. "The case is over and we won two out of three! The jury found that your employee was in fact the technology's inventor. The jury also found that your patent is valid. The only adverse result was the jury's finding that you irrevocably transferred all of your rights in the technology to the plaintiff." Which of course meant that we wouldn't be able to use the technology until we made a deal with the plaintiff, which temporarily could bring to an end a very profitable product line. In a way, I felt like it was my fault. I thought it should have been obvious that the Company's overriding objective was to be able to continue to use the technology. I should have had a discussion about the Company's objectives before I hired that outside counsel. My particular solution was never to hire him again, but as solutions go, this one was, to say the least, a little late.

- **Hire outside counsel who are as committed as you are.**
There is an old joke about commitment. It involves a project
consisting of a plate of ham and eggs. The punchline is that the
chicken, who contributed the eggs to the plate, was interested
in the project. But the pig was committed! The joke offers an
extreme example. But commitment is critical, especially in
your biggest lawsuits where your company is the defendant.
To be sure, sometimes the job of an outside counsel is to tell
you have a bad case, a sure loser. You should respect that.
You should listen. You should ask questions. And then you
should decide whether you believe they are right. Keep in mind
that most of the time they are right. But if you don't agree, if
you think the case can end in a better way, you need to face
up to the fact that you now have two choices. Either change
the mind of your outside counsel. Or fire them. There's no
third way. I recommend firing them. You can sell yourself on
the idea that your outside counsel is a professional, that he
or she will put forth the same level of effort and devote the
same amount of thought to your defense as you would get if
your outside counsel thought you had a chance to win. But
experience taught me that you can't count on it. Ask yourself
this. Suppose you have cancer. You interview two doctors. The
first doctor tells you your cancer is terminal. This first doctor
advises that he or she will follow the normal regimen in a case
like yours, including radiation, chemotherapy, surgery, etc. But
you will die nevertheless. The second doctor acknowledges the
seriousness of your cancer, but tells you that you should not
give up, that he or she will do everything possible to produce
the best outcome for you. And will keep fighting for you as long
as you are willing to keep fighting for yourself. Everything
else being equal in the doctors' backgrounds and experience,
who will you pick? I respect whichever choice you make.
The first choice emphasizes reality and objectivity, mixed in
with a little fatalism. The second choice emphasizes hope and
determination, and perhaps a little unwarranted optimism.

Whichever choice you make, you need a committed outside counsel. Which one is more committed? Here are some telltale signs to help you spot the outside counsel who may not be as committed to your case as you are.

- o First, be wary of a litigation defense plan that looks like what I would refer to as "the standard playbook". In the standard playbook approach, your outside counsel files a motion to dismiss, followed by an answer, followed by discovery, followed by a motion for summary judgment, followed by consideration of settlement (if not sooner), followed by trial, followed by appeal. If that is all you see in the plan, if there is nothing innovative, no strategies to turn the case around, to recast it, whether through counterclaims, or venue transfers, or some other tactic to improve your chances of winning, then you are seeing a plan without the aggressiveness that is fueled by hope and commitment. Your outside counsel is the interested chicken.

- o Second, if possible, pay attention to how your outside counsel talks about the case, especially to the judge. I received some great advice on this point from one of my outside counsel. He said, "I listen to what the associates on my team say to the judge. There is a tremendous difference in attitude between someone who starts with 'Your Honor, it is my client's position that...' and someone who says, "Your Honor, we believe that...'. I only want the latter kind of lawyers on the team that represents you. They are the lawyers who have adopted your cause as their cause." You have to have a good ear to hear that difference but it's worth listening for.

- **Take extra time when you hire outside counsel to investigate you.** You might be able to go through an entire career as General Counsel and never have to hire an outside counsel to do an independent internal investigation at your company. But if you do, chances are that the outside counsel you will consider hiring will be a lawyer who used to be a prosecutor. I had lots of experience in retaining outside counsel to do internal investigations. The reasons were many and varied, and beside the point. What I did find was that all of the former prosecutors with whom I worked were very good lawyers. They also were very good investigators. And the very best of them had the same objective I had, which was to find the truth, good or bad. It is imperative that you find the very best of them. Because you must keep in mind that once you hire an outside counsel to do an independent investigation, you surrender your right to supervise their work. You have to be sure they are as willing to conclude that your client is innocent as they are willing to conclude that your client is guilty. I know he is fictional, but if you can, you should hire that prosecutor from the movie, "My Cousin Vinnie", the one who voluntarily moves to dismiss his case once he sees that Joe Pesci's clients undoubtedly are innocent.

Professional baseball teams have been searching for that perfect data base for years, one that will tell them who is the best hitter against a particular pitcher, where your fielders should stand based on who is at bat, when it's time to bring in a relief pitcher from your bullpen. etc. In the meantime, they are stuck with having to make intelligent baseball decisions.

Someday there will be an app available to in-house lawyers. It will include a data base filled with historical information about every outside counsel everywhere. The information will include detailed histories of their results, not just wins and losses, but all outcomes. The data base will show who were the associates who assisted them, unique aspects of the cases handled by them, how much they charged, who were the opposing lawyers, and on and on. In-house lawyers will be able simply to enter data concerning their particular matter, and the app will tell them who they should hire.

In the meantime, you are stuck with having to make intelligent decisions. But look on the bright side. At least your choices won't be shown on national TV and second guessed on ESPN.

CHAPTER 21

Learn The Things That You Think Won't Be On The Test

My predecessor as General Counsel came to Navistar following a successful career as an in-house lawyer at another company, a company whose products were not motor vehicles. Unlike Navistar, his former company's products were not distributed through independently owned vehicle dealers. As a result, he had no prior experience with state motor vehicle dealer termination laws.

During his 14 years at Navistar, the biggest litigation loss on which he had to report to the Board of Directors was a $25 million judgment against the Company in a dealer termination lawsuit.

At the first Board of Directors meeting I attended after becoming General Counsel, I had to tell the directors about a major piece of litigation involving intellectual property disputes between the Company and one of our largest suppliers, a dispute that threatened the very continuation of one of our products. By that time in my career I had had significant experience in contract law, financing transactions, bankruptcy, securities law, mergers and acquisitions, labor and employment, employee benefits law, state and federal tax law, Delaware corporation law, real estate, environmental law, and yes, dealer termination laws. Almost every area of the law.

Except intellectual property law.

My successor's first big report to the Navistar Board of Directors was to inform them about a big litigation loss in a warranty lawsuit. You guessed it. He had practically no experience in warranty cases.

The legal areas in which you practice before you become General Counsel are hard enough as it is. Every legal area is constantly evolving. New laws are passed. New regulations are adopted. New court rulings pose new challenges. But there is no getting around the fact that if you are going to be the General Counsel, you must have a certain amount of expertise in all legal areas, not just the ones you have practiced on a daily basis.

Candidly, I don't know the best way for you to broaden your legal skills portfolio. My broadening took place almost by accident. I started out as a labor and employment lawyer. Then the Company needed to sell a bunch of businesses, so I learned how to do that. Then environmental law became a hot topic, and so I learned that. Then, because of a death in the Law Department, I moved on to real estate. Then the finance and securities lawyer left the Company and I replaced him. And so on. It almost seems like my advice should be to work in-house at a company that has a lot of problems and lots of turnover. I have no doubt that problems and turnovers created my opportunities. But I am sure there are better ways.

After I became General Counsel, I thought I should try to find some of those better ways to help the lawyers on my staff get ready for my job. I tried three things. They had, as we corporate types like to say about our mostly unsuccessful experiments, mixed results.

First, I held a monthly meeting with all of the attorneys in the Law Department. The agenda for each meeting was what might be called a "deep dive" into a matter or matters being handled by one or more of the Law Department attorneys. The deep dive provided an opportunity for the rest of the attorneys to learn about a practice area where they had either limited experience or no experience.

The meeting time every month was at noon. We referred to it as the "brown bag lunch". This approach may have been more helpful than I thought at the time. But I do have to say that on the occasions when I provided free pizza for the group, attendance was a lot better. They seemed very hungry for pizza and less so for knowledge of legal areas outside their assigned responsibilities.

Also, at the end of one of the brown bag meetings, when, like I always did, I asked if anyone had any questions, one of the lawyers raised his hand and asked, "Will this be on the test?" In fairness to him, he had a much-appreciated sense of humor, and his "question" was humorously delivered. Plus he had no aspirations to be the General Counsel.

Second, on more than one occasion, I met with the practice group leaders who reported directly to me and suggested that we implement a program of rotating the attorneys on their staff from one practice group to another in order to enhance their skills and make them more promotable, whether they ultimately were General Counsel candidates or not. Employment attorneys could try out credit and collection law. Product litigation attorneys could rotate into the group that did mergers and acquisitions. And so forth.

My suggestion always went nowhere. I understood why and I sympathized with my staff. Their lives were difficult enough without having to take on the extra burden of temporarily losing their best attorneys to another practice group, and at the same time taking on still another extra burden of training the attorney who rotated into their group.

Third, on a bi-weekly basis, I held staff meetings attended by those same attorneys who headed up the various practice groups in the Law Department and who reported directly to me. At the staff meetings, each practice group head reported on the five or six significant matters being handled in his or her group. The meetings lasted several hours. They were very helpful for me. I learned a lot by listening to the reports and asking questions. It also was an opportunity for the other members of my staff to see the wider picture of the Law Department and learn more about all of the legal practice areas in it.

I hoped that the meetings would help prepare the members of my staff to be General Counsels, whether at Navistar or somewhere else. I believe that it was a help, although I have to confess that on more than one occasion, I looked across the conference table at the lawyer who, as it turned out, eventually succeeded me, and noticed with chagrin that he was reading and responding to emails on his iPhone during other lawyers' reports. Later, when he had to go tell the Board of Directors about that big warranty lawsuit loss, I wondered if he regretted not paying more attention to the reports on warranty cases that he didn't listen to in those staff meetings. Probably not. Whether it was warranty law or any other area, he was a very quick learner. How fast do you learn?

You might think that, once you are General Counsel, the limits of what you need to know stop at the borders of the Law Department. If so, you should think again. It is true that a successful General Counsel must have a lot more than just a casual acquaintance with every area of the law handled in the Law Department. But that is just the beginning. In fact, it is what some people call "table stakes".

As General Counsel, it is very likely that you also will be an executive officer. That title brings additional responsibilities. It becomes a given that you understand the business, an understanding that exceeds general knowledge of the company's products. The General Counsel ends up communicating with more third parties than anyone else on his or her staff. Whether they are potential lenders, investment bankers, board members, government regulators, joint venture partners, or shareholder advisory firms, third parties have more confidence in you if they feel that you understand the whole company, not just its legal issues.

Once I conducted an impromptu survey of my General Counsel colleagues at a roundtable meeting for General Counsels of manufacturing companies. I showed them a list of the various disciplines that were common to all of our corporations, including engineering, Information Technology, manufacturing, human resources, distribution, accounting, treasury, sales, marketing, internal audit, external communications, and shareholder relations. I asked them to provide a ranking of how proficient they needed to be in each discipline, on a scale from 1 (clueless) to 10 (you could do the job better than any of the incumbents currently working in that discipline).

I had been a General Counsel for a while by this time, and so their answers didn't surprise me, but they might surprise you. About 20 General Counsels each provided a ranking for each discipline. Discipline by discipline, not one General Counsel provided a single ranking of less than 3. There were some 4s and 5s, but most of their rankings were in the 6 to 8 range. There were a few 9s. Taken as a whole, the average ranking they gave in each discipline ranged from 6 to just under 8.

I had to explain to investment bankers why the paint we used in painting our trucks had to have such high levels of volatile organic compounds. I also had to explain what volatile organic compounds were.

I had to explain to some other investment bankers the calculation and uses of engine emission credits to meet diesel engine emissions rules.

I had to explain to a group of lenders how a reverse subsidiary merger worked.

I had to explain to several U.S. Congressmen and one U.S. Senator the difference between selective catalytic reduction and exhaust gas recirculation as methods for controlling nitrogen oxide emissions from truck tailpipes.

I didn't think any of those items ever would have been on my test. But they were. And there were others.

What will be on your test? I suppose you could wait and see. But I recommend that you don't take more chances than you need to take. Learn the things that you think won't be on the test.

CHAPTER 22

Join a Club

I don't mean a country club. You can do that if you want to. I'm sure it doesn't hurt. But what I am referring to is a club for General Counsels.

I participated in a group of General Counsels that met on a regular basis. We used our meetings to benchmark with each other and learn about new legal trends. Also, during the meeting breaks, we commiserated with each other about how hard our jobs were. Always a source of comfort.

At each meeting there were speakers. Sometimes our speakers were lawyers from law firms who made presentations about their specialties. More often, our speakers were General Counsels who were members of our group. The feedback from the group was that they got more out of the presentations from their fellow General Counsels than from the law firm speakers.

General Counsels have very unique jobs. I recommend that you find and join a group of General Counsels that meet on a regular basis. The people who can help you be the best General Counsel you can be are other General Counsels. They do the same job you do. In any group of them, chances are very good that whatever problem you have is one that they have already experienced. The best of them will share how they handled their version of that particular problem. And by and large, they will not pretend that they found the perfect solution, nor that their solution would work every time.

Just before I became Navistar's General Counsel, I had lunch with a General Counsel who'd served in that role at a retailer that was a much larger company than Navistar. He gave me some good advice. He talked about achieving perfection. He said, "Steve, I learned that I had to be comfortable with the fact that every day, somewhere in the company, we were violating some law. It is inevitable. The business people try their best, but they aren't lawyers. And I didn't have enough lawyers, and in fact there's no way I could have had enough lawyers, to preview every action before it was taken. A big part of the job is fixing mistakes, and trying to minimize the chances that those particular mistakes get made again and again, because that's where punitive damages come from."

Another General Counsel put it in this way. "The job of the General Counsel is like the job of that guy who follows behind the circus parade, cleaning up after the elephants." Earthy, but more or less true.

Another benefit of joining a General Counsel group is that your fellow GCs will have faced problems that you haven't faced yet, but that might be heading your way. Listen to their stories. Even if you think their problem won't be a problem that you will have to face as General Counsel at your company, listen anyway. You never know. They probably didn't expect their particular problem was one they were going to have to face.

As you look for that group of General Counsels to join, make sure they really are General Counsels. Sometimes a group is advertised as a General Counsel discussion group, and you find that many of the members are law department deputy general counsels, the second-in-commands. I have nothing against second-in-commands. I used to be one. Many of them go on to become successful General Counsels. But while they are still second-in-commands, they tend to talk like know-it-alls. It seems to come with the job.

I have been in more than one "General Counsel" discussion group meeting where I sought advice on a challenge I faced in my Law Department, only to have someone tell me with great assurance that at his or her company they don't have that problem because of some program they instituted that was a tremendous success. Just from the description of the program, I could tell I was listening to a second-in-command. I knew that the program couldn't possibly be as successful as they were making it sound.

I don't know why second-in-commands tend to be that way. Maybe it's because they don't yet have the biggest job in the law department, and they think that to get it they have to act supremely self-confident. Maybe they are right. But all of the useful advice I ever received on general counselling came from veteran General Counsels, who'd learned that their jobs included successes that were nevertheless not perfect, and failures that taught them how to do better next time.

I thought I had found a perfect General Counsel group. The group met every other month for dinner. At one of the dinners I sat next to the General Counsel of a Fortune 1000 public company. She told me about all of the things she was doing in her law department and how well everything was working. Everything. It was clear she had it all figured out. I was surprised. I almost was tempted to start taking notes. But as we continued to talk, she told me about successful things she was doing that I knew from personal experience couldn't be going that well. We talked a little more. I asked her how long she had been General Counsel.

"I was named General Counsel two months ago."

"And what was your role before becoming the GC?" I asked.

"I was the deputy general counsel."

I made a mental note to check back with her in three or four years. And in the meantime, to sit next to someone else at dinner.

CHAPTER 23

Talk Last

When I was growing up, I knew someone who was a quiet and reserved man. I remember once someone asked him why. He said, "I think it's better to listen. If someone talks, and I listen, then when they're done talking, I know what they know. And I already know what I know."

I'm not that quiet. But I thought there was a lesson in that approach that was worth keeping in mind.

General Counsels should talk last whenever possible. You may have gotten the job by speaking up, but now you've got the job. And part of the job is shutting up. And listening before speaking.

There are lots of reasons to talk last. Here are some of them.

General Counsels attend a lot of meetings where the lawyers on their staff, and the outside lawyers, gather to discuss "what to do next" on a particular matter. Everyone who attends those meetings knows that the final decision belongs to the General Counsel. But in every meeting I attended with other lawyers, both from the Law Department and from our outside law firms, I tried to remember to go around the room and ask every person to say what he or she thought we should do next before announcing a decision. Here's why:

- It gives you more time to think. The decisions that you have to make as General Counsel tend to be hard, and they tend to be big. If they were simple and small, you probably wouldn't even be in the meeting.

- It is likely that you will have entered the meeting with your own opinion as to what to do. But if you talk last, and in the meantime if you are a good listener, you may hear something that will change your mind. That happened to me more times than I would care to admit.

- Even if you enter the meeting with a firm opinion as to what to do next, and even if that opinion doesn't change by the end of the meeting, you will still benefit from talking last. As you listen to each lawyer talk, you will find out who you are going to be agreeing with and who you are going to be overruling. Whenever I talked last and informed everyone of what I wanted to do next, I tried to make sure I acknowledged the validity of the point of view of the lawyer or lawyers who were being overruled. Even if you are not following the advice of one of your lawyers, it's important for them to feel like they've been heard. And if it happens that your decision turns out to be wrong, and their recommendation would have produced a better result, you get an opportunity to tell them they were right. Most people like to hear that. Especially from the boss.

- Asking for everyone's opinion, and reserving judgment until everyone has had their chance to talk, provides a useful data point in evaluating your outside counsel. In meetings attended by more than one lawyer from one of our outside law firms, I always listened carefully to what the junior associate said. Sometimes the associate merely restated or parroted what the partner said. Sometimes it was clear that the associate was an independent thinker and didn't feel that he or she had to agree

100% with the partner. Generally speaking, associates in the latter category worked in firms that were overall better firms.

- If everyone in the meeting agrees with each other, and if you agree with them, then you don't even have to talk. And you have to talk enough as it is.

A big reason to talk last is that, once you become General Counsel, you will find that people who work for you will be reluctant to disagree with you. You can preach openness and tolerance for alternative viewpoints all you want, but the reality of any law department, including your law department and mine, is that once the General Counsel gives his or her opinion, discussion tends to stop. And most people are reluctant to tell the boss when they think he or she is wrong.

I once was organizing a meeting. The meeting was with some government officials in a nearby city. The Company representatives going with me to the meeting would be a lawyer on my staff, two environmental compliance managers, and one of the Company's executive officers. The plan was for the Company representatives to meet at a hotel just off the expressway and then drive together to the nearby city. Everyone except the executive officer who was going with us lived near the expressway exit where we had agreed to meet. The executive officer lived in a suburb some distance away from the rendezvous expressway exit.

On the day before the trip, we met to discuss our plans for the meeting and to go over the logistics. The executive officer said he was unfamiliar with the expressway exit and asked for directions. (This was before widespread GPS use.) I forgot to talk last. I immediately replied, telling him that he should get on the southbound expressway near his home, then follow the signs to the westbound expressway. I told him that once he got on the westbound expressway, he would reach the exit where he was to meet us "in about two miles".

The actual distance was 9 ½ miles.

The next day, we waited at the hotel for him. He arrived late. He said he almost turned around when he didn't see the exit where I told him it would be. He was irritated. I didn't blame him. Later I asked the lawyer on my staff, "When I said yesterday that he would be exiting the expressway in about 2 miles, did you know the distance to that expressway exit was close to 10 miles"? "Yes," she replied. "But I didn't want to contradict you in front of the client." I wanted to be angry with her. But I knew who was at fault, and it wasn't her.

There is also good reason to talk last in settings other than ones where the meeting participants are the lawyers who work for you.

The General Counsel usually attends the meetings of senior management. Lots of topics are discussed. Usually the purpose of the discussion on a particular topic is to arrive at a decision. Sometimes, as you listen to a particular discussion, you will hear an idea that, for whatever reason, would raise legal issues that make the idea a bad idea. You may be tempted to speak up immediately to pour your legal cold water on the idea. But if you are as fortunate as I was, your senior management colleagues may be as smart as the ones with whom I worked. And if so, one or more of them may identify the idea as a bad idea, or suggest an alternative version of the idea that cures your legal concerns. And what happens in those moments is you have avoided the need to be the one who says no. Believe me, you'll get to say no often enough.

One caveat is worth remembering. If the CEO is good at the job, he or she will want to be the one who talks last. In those settings, you should try to talk second to last.

Talking last isn't a cure-all for everything. Sometimes everyone in the meeting will agree with each other, and you don't agree with any of them. Even at those times, it's good to talk last, because at least you know what you're up against.

I once attended a mediation session for a very big case. Our legal team was large. Five outside lawyers. Two lawyers from my staff. And me. It was a typical mediation setting. The legal team for Navistar was in one room. Lawyers representing our opponents were in another room.

The mediator met first with the other side. Then he came into our room and informed us of the settlement demand from the other side.

They wanted somewhere around $39 million. That number was about 5% of what, according to their calculations, they would recover if they won the case. The mediator said it was a good deal and we should strongly consider taking it.

The mediator left the room so we could discuss the offer. I went around the room and asked each person for their thoughts. Each member of the team had a slightly different idea of how we should respond, but everyone thought the offer was a good one. Most people thought we should make a counter-offer in the low $30 millions. One person thought our counter-offer should be in the $20 million range. I made sure to thank everyone for their input. Then I called the mediator back into the room. I offered $2 million. The mediation ended about five minutes later.

We resumed settlement discussions several weeks later. The case eventually settled for about $14 million.

To be clear, I didn't think that the other lawyers on my team had been wrong in suggesting we offer more. The case was a class action case. Navistar was the defendant. I have yet to meet an outside counsel who didn't preach early and often the value of settling class actions. Continuing to defend a class action case is a risky proposition because the stakes are so high. It was risky to offer $2 million and let the opponents walk out of the mediation. The outside counsel you hire aren't there to take big risks.

Taking big risks is your job. And just one more reason to talk last.

CHAPTER 24

Stay Calm – Or at Least
Act Like You Are

When you are the General Counsel, there seem to be unlimited opportunities to panic. Here were some of mine.

"The jury just announced an eight-figure verdict against the Company."

"FBI agents are in the front lobby."

"The U.S. Attorney is on the phone and wants to talk to you."

It is no exaggeration to say that how you respond to events like that define whether or not you will be a successful General Counsel.

A few years before I became General Counsel, I worked with an executive coach. Navistar was going through a phase where executive coaches were in vogue, and so I had one. Mine was from Human Resources. He interviewed me and then followed me around during the day while I worked, and he watched. I thought at the time that he had a pretty easy job, watching someone else work.

He gave me two pieces of advice, at least two that I remembered.

One was that I should sit up straighter. He said I slouched when I sat. He said it made me look judgmental, and looking judgmental would have a negative effect on the people who reported to me. He said he thought I was judgmental enough without looking even more judgmental by slouching. I told him my judgment was that he was wrong. He didn't laugh. You don't find a lot of people with a sense of humor in the executive coaching business.

I tried to follow his advice. But I forgot to sit up straight way more often than I remembered.

My coach's other advice struck a nerve and triggered a memory. At one of our sessions, he said to me, "Steve, I have noticed that you walk too fast."

"I walk too fast?"

"Yes. You walk too fast."

"OK," I said. "But, look. I'm busy. I have lots of things to do. You must have noticed that. You are not saying that I rush to judgment or cut corners when I'm working, right? Because I would agree that would be a bad thing. But I am not working when I am walking from one place to another. I'm just getting to where I'm going. So what's wrong with walking fast?"

Other arguments were forming in my mind as I spoke. One was about how it had to be a good thing for leaders to project energy, and walking fast did that. I was leading by example. Yeah, that's it. Leading by example.

My coach interrupted these thoughts by saying, "Leaders need to be approachable. How approachable do you think you are?"

He was right. How many times had someone come up to me and begun a conversation by saying, "Steve, I know you're busy, but…"? I always thought that just meant they knew what I already knew, namely, that I was busy. But it also meant something else.

"I have seen more than one instance when you walked right past someone who was trying to get your attention," my coach explained. "You missed seeing them. Because you were focused on where you were going, not where you were. Even more important, you are making them decide whether whatever they want to say to you is important enough to interrupt you when you appear to be in such a hurry."

By this time, since I already agreed with him, I was barely listening. My mind had drifted back to my first job after college. I was a teller supervisor in a savings and loan association. It was the 1970s. The Great Depression of the 1930s had ended decades before. But the executive officers who ran the savings and loan remembered the Depression. So did many of the savings and loan's customers. One of their memories was of bank failures, of frantic people trying to get their money out of savings institutions that were closing their doors for good. It was called a run on the bank. The executives remembered.

So they had a rule. Nobody in the savings and loan, especially the supervisors, was ever supposed to hurry. Ever. Our job was to project calm, to show our customers that everything was under control. We were told to do that even if things weren't under control.

For example, at each teller station, there was a silent alarm in the form of a button under the counter. In the event of a robbery, the teller was supposed to push the button. The button alerted the telephone operators, whose job was to call the police, and then do a public address announcement using a special code. The code was to announce that there was a call for "Mr. Vare." There was no Mr. Vare. The announcement meant a robbery was in progress. When we supervisors heard that announcement, we were supposed to move toward the teller area, if we weren't already there, so that we might be able to help provide a description of the robber. *But even then, we couldn't hurry.* I guess the feeling was that it was better for the robber to get away than for one of us to look panicky and trigger a run by the customers.

After that conversation with my coach, I tried to walk more slowly.

My first executive coach wasn't my last one. I had another one after I became General Counsel. At one of our first meetings, he told me a story.

"I once worked as an executive coach at a large manufacturing company," he said. "The CEO of the company was approaching retirement. It was time to identify a succession candidate. The CEO thought his replacement should be the CFO. The CEO talked with several board members about the prospect of the CFO becoming the next CEO. Each director he talked with was cool to the idea."

"The CEO asked me to find out why. I contacted the directors and met with them in private to find out why they were hesitant to promote the CFO to CEO. They were candid and provided very useful feedback. Each one offered a similar assessment. As one of them put it, 'The directors always meet for dinner on the night before each board meeting. When the CEO joins us, he is relaxed, he projects an air of confidence, and as he chats with us before and during dinner, he tells us about his excitement over what we are going to see and hear at tomorrow's board meeting. In contrast, the CFO is always late, comes rushing in holding papers in one hand and his cell phone in the other. His tie is slightly askew. He is the perfect embodiment of a harried man. Why would we give that man a bigger job?'"

By this time, I was getting more accustomed to executive coaches, and so my coach didn't have to tell me that the story was really about me. Before I became General Counsel, I was the Corporate Secretary. As Corporate Secretary, one of my tasks was to organize, and then attend, the director dinners held before each Navistar board meeting. I was usually late. I was usually just finishing a phone call as I walked into the dining room. I can say that my tie was never askew, but so what? The rest of the description completely fit the person I had been before becoming General Counsel.

I can say that I was already in the process of at least appearing to be calm, relaxed and in control, but that story from my executive coach was a helpful reinforcement. Several years later I was sitting in an airport in Mexico City. One of my peers at Navistar was sitting next to me. He confided in me that his career goal was to be promoted to the job held by his boss. He asked me if I thought he had a chance to get it.

It was the only time I was called upon to be someone else's executive coach. I decided to be blunt.

"I strongly doubt it," I told him.

"Why do you think so?" he said, the disappointment showing on his face.

I said, "Let me explain by asking you a couple of questions. First, how many hours a week do you work?"

"Somewhere between 70 and 80," he said, with obvious pride.

"How often do you come into the office on Sunday?"

"I am in the office for most of the day almost every Sunday."

"And does your boss know that?" I asked.

"Yes. Once in a while, he comes in for a short time on Sunday, so he sees me."

"And does the rest of your staff also come in every Sunday?"

"Well, no," he replied. "I believe that they deserve some rest and I don't want to create a working environment where burnout and turnover become problems."

"It's good that you care about your staff," I told him, "but what your boss sees is that you are doing work that arguably should be done by the people who report to you. He also sees that to get your current job done you have to work up to 80 hours every week. In short, what he sees is someone who is barely able to handle his current job but nevertheless wants an even bigger job."

I would like to be able to end that story by reporting that my coaching worked, that my colleague changed his ways and eventually got the bigger job. But he didn't change. And he never got the bigger job.

General Counsels have to project calm, have to display grace under pressure, have to communicate through everything they say and do that they are firmly in control of whatever it is. The Board of Directors gets limited opportunities to see their General Counsel. Generally, they are not lawyers. So the way they judge you is mostly on your results, but partly on whether they think you can handle the company's legal affairs, whether you project the calm and self- confidence that tells them you know what you're doing and have things under control.

Members of senior management, also non-lawyers, may get to see you more often, but their confidence in you is greatly enhanced if you never seem panicky. And the people in your law department? They need your calm most of all. If you still need to ask why, you should stop reading now.

If you remember nothing else about staying calm, just remember this one thing. Walk slower. That's not the entire recipe, but it helps. And take heart. I can tell you from personal experience that, as you get older, walking slowly comes more naturally.

CHAPTER 25

Be A Decathlete

The decathlon is a Summer Olympics event. It features 10 different events over a two day time period. Decathletes have to compete in all 10 events. They can't win unless they do.

One of the adages of corporate life says that at the highest level of the corporation, which includes the General Counsel, it is perfectly acceptable to completely lack a particular skill, even more than one. The adage says that you can compensate for these skill gaps by "surrounding yourself with the right people" who, presumably, possess the skills you lack. All you need is the wisdom to know your own weaknesses and the ability to spot the people who can fill in your skill gaps. Then it's just a matter of delegation.

Most adages have some truth in them. But as adages go, I would put this one in the "urban myth" category. There are some things you have to do yourself. Whether you are good at doing them or mediocre at doing them, you have to do them. Some things can't be delegated. At least they shouldn't be.

Some executives, and some would-be executives, insist that there are no non-delegable tasks, that the only thing necessary for success in the top job is "being a leader", by which these particular people mean "having a big job title and getting paid lots of money". They tell themselves that, just by coincidence, the things they don't do well are not all that important. Therefore, it's ok, they say in justification, to completely skip doing them. In my experience, the people who believe that usually don't get the big jobs, and if they do, they usually don't stay in them for very long.

Here is a partial list of General Counsel decathlon events that I firmly believe you have to show up for, things you have to do yourself.

- **Speaking to large groups of people.** I once worked with an otherwise excellent attorney who suffered from what I can only call stage fright. The attorney was bright and, in very small groups, comfortable and articulate. He was an excellent lawyer whose clients within the Company had great respect for him. However, on the occasions when he was called upon to speak in front of a large group of Company employees, his nervousness was vividly on display. He stumbled through whatever presentation he was making. Worse still, when members of the audience asked questions, he was so nervous that he struggled to understand the question and sometimes ended up answering another question, not the one that had been asked. The General Counsel sometimes has to speak to the entire Law Department. You are making a mistake if you never do that. The General Counsel also has to speak at Board of Directors meetings. That can't be delegated. There may come a time in the future when all meetings are online, and all presentations take place via skype. Until then, speaking to large groups of people is a must.

- **Standing up to senior management.** You can have a great relationship with all of the members of the senior management team, including the CEO. And you might get lucky. You might complete an entire career as General Counsel and never have to stand alone and insist that your management can't do what they want to do. Maybe. But I had a great relationship with all of the CEOs with whom I worked. I was lucky that I could agree with them almost all of the time. And still, on more than one occasion, I reached a point where I had to say that if the management was going to take a particular action, I would have to have a discussion about it with the Board of Directors. When I had those tough conversations, I was lucky. Senior management on each occasion was willing to listen and to find another way. Standing up to senior management sounds like one of those catch phrases that simply means being oppositional and saying no. It isn't. It is its own skill. It consists of being able to educate, to persuade, combined with a willingness to listen and not just be obstinate, and, most of all, the ability to know the difference between disagreeing with management and needing to oppose management. And it goes without saying that when it comes to standing up to senior management, the General Counsel can't send someone else to do it.

- **Making decisions.** It is the nature of the job. General Counsel decision making is a skill that has a lot of sub-skills, like gathering information, knowing when you have more time to decide and when you have to make an immediate decision, taking advice from others, and of course, making the right decision. You will find as General Counsel that some people on your staff, even experienced attorneys, will push decisions at you and make the responsibility yours alone. I called it the "make you aware" syndrome. Whenever one of the lawyers on my staff came to me and opened the conversation by saying, "I want to make you aware...", it was a sure sign they were facing a difficult problem that needed a decision and either they didn't want to make the decision, or they couldn't make the decision. As General Counsel, you don't get that choice. Believe it or not, you can get pretty far in a law department without having to make decisions. I have known many successful in-house attorneys who made sure that someone else, usually their clients, made all of the decisions. They provided the legal advice and the client made their choice. They were successful lawyers. Not one of them ever became a General Counsel.

- **Triaging.** Triaging sounds like a medical term, but it applies to General Counsels also. Triaging is the process of deciding where to put your departmental resources and where to put your personal time and energy. I don't know how doctors do triage. It probably has something to do with blood loss and vital signs. I do know how General Counsels do it, although it is a difficult process to explain. Some matters look like they will be enterprise threatening, and they aren't. Other matters have small beginnings but eventually will grow very large and get out of hand because of inattention. You have to know the difference. It starts with listening carefully and critically, not just when new matters arrive in the Law Department, but also when developments occur in ongoing matters. That listening has to be accompanied by evaluation. You have to answer the question for yourself, is this a matter that needs different attention than it will otherwise get if I don't act to provide the extra attention? That evaluation requires that you know the law that will apply. You also have to know the parties involved, both on the other side of the table and on your side. Thorough triaging also may require knowing about the judge in the case, about what kind of jurors you can expect and other factors. It also requires that you know the lawyers on your staff, how they will handle the matter if you leave it all up to them. You have to able to anticipate what will happen next, and what will happen after that. Then you have to decide whether a particular matter needs more attention than it otherwise would get. To be sure, triaging is also done by the lawyers who report to you. But it remains true that the person who is in the best position to see all of the cases and know how all of the resources are deployed is you. Just like in medicine, not all law department cases require a Code Blue and a life-saving team with a crash cart. But when they do, you have to be the person who sounds the alarm, not the one who merely hears it over the intercom.

- **Making your Law Department diverse.** By the time you become General Counsel you should have figured out that diversity makes your Law Department better. Put another way, you should know that your Law Department will never be as good as it could be if it lacks diversity. Making your Law Department diverse, being the strongest champion of diversity, is one of the things you have to do. Lip service in this area does not work. During my time as General Counsel, there was no template for achieving diversity. I tried a lot of different things. Some seemed to have good effects. Some didn't. The biggest lesson I learned was the importance of not giving up. The good news about diversity is that if you keep trying, and you make sincere efforts, you will succeed. In the Navistar Law Department I led, over half of my direct reports were women. Just under half of my direct reports were minorities. The numbers varied from time to time, but about 45% of the lawyers in the Navistar Law Department were women and just under 20% were minorities. Both percentages were substantially above the percentages of women and minorities in the legal profession as a whole. I sometimes read about awards given to other law departments for the diversity they had achieved. Sometimes my diversity data were better than those of the award recipients. If I could do it over again, I might have tried to get those diversity awards. My advice is to go after the awards if you think that will help make your law department more diverse. But whatever you do, keep at it. Diversity offers performance excellence that your law department must have in order to be a success. And only you can make it happen.

- **Recruitment and development.** On your worst days as General Counsel, you may feel like baseball manager Casey Stengel, who once said about the struggling team he was managing, "Can't anybody here play this game?" It may seem to you that you are the only lawyer in your law department who knows what they're doing, that you are doing all the thinking that's being done. If that happens, I can tell you something that will make you feel even worse. Those feelings you are having simply mean that you are not doing your job well. If you were, your people would be better. Like all other managers, General Counsels have to hire the best people they can find. And once they hire them, they have to help them develop their skills to a higher level. The main reason for triaging is that you can't be everywhere and involved in everything. The main reason for doing a good job at recruiting and developing the people on your staff is the same. I have no advice for you regarding how to make the best hiring decisions and how to be the best talent developer. As General Counsel decathlons go, recruitment and development were not my strongest events. But I worked hard at it and over time I got better. Here are a few things I learned along the way.

    o   Try not to hire people who are exactly like you. If everyone in the Law Department was just like you, everyone would be bad at the things you're bad at. And there would be too much group-think because everyone would see things exactly the way you see them.

    o   Recognize that professional development is in the eye of the beholder. Some attorneys relish the opportunity to expand their practice portfolio and learn new areas of the law. Others don't. Their idea of professional development is to get better at what they currently are doing. It took me a while to realize both kinds of attorneys are choosing the right thing for them, and that the General Counsel's job is to identify who is in which category and work to provide the right growth opportunities for each.

o   Respect the decisions your attorneys make about their continuing legal education. You may have a much different idea about the best CLE for the members of your staff. But as long as they remain interested in their own professional development, and as long as their choices are not exclusively seminars in Hawaii, the decision should be theirs, not yours. You make enough decisions as it is.

o   If a development plan for a particular attorney isn't working, change the plan. Don't give up. Sometimes you put someone in a job and then find that they are not succeeding. At those times, it's good to remember that you put them there. And that means you have the responsibility to restructure, or reassign, or re-whatever you have to do to put them in a job where they can succeed. You both will be happier.

- **Firing people.** Firing people is difficult. It is among the most emotion-laden things you have to do as General Counsel. I have known managers who just could not bring themselves to do it. They had to have someone from Human Resources fire people for them. If you are lucky, and if you are excellent at talent selection in the first instance, you shouldn't have to fire too many people during your tenure as General Counsel. But the chances that you will never have to fire anyone are, as the saying goes, slim to none. There are plenty of articles that will give you best practices for how to terminate an employee. I will only mention the three tips that were especially helpful to me.

o   First, don't think of what you are doing as doling out punishment. It may feel that way. But the reality is that the person you are firing may just be in the wrong job and you don't have the right one to offer to them. I fired one person who later became very successful in a completely different field, doing a job that did not exist anywhere at Navistar.

o   Second, don't spend a lot of time discussing the reasons for your decision. If you have done things right and provided ample feedback and warnings, the decision shouldn't be a big surprise to the person you are firing. And if you haven't done things right, now is not the time to have that discussion. It's too late. You are announcing a decision already made, not having a discussion about it. Of course, people have the right to know your reasons, but the less time you spend in that mode, the better.

o   Finally, and, for me, most importantly, tell the person that you are terminating them within the first 10 seconds after the meeting begins. I always found that firing people was stressful. I dreaded the termination meeting. My pulse rate went up as soon as the person walked into my office. But I read somewhere that if you inform the person right away that you are firing them, your nervousness will subside and you will handle the rest of the meeting better. It worked for me. I passed that advice along to the managing attorneys on my staff. It had a humorous consequence. Often when I called one of them to my office to discuss something, he or she would glance at their watch moments after sitting down to talk with me and quip, "Well, I've been here for 10 seconds and you haven't fired me, so I guess whatever it is, at least my job is safe."

If you have been keeping score, you know that my General Counsel decathlon list has only seven events, not ten. My reaction to that is, first, you're being a little nit-picky, don't you think? Second, my list of seven events gives you the opportunity to add your own three items. Unlike the Summer Olympics decathlon, the decathlon for a General Counsel will vary a little based on who we are and which company we work for.

Your additional three events might include successfully dealing with Law Department attorneys in countries other than your own.

You might add as an event the creation and successful defense of your departmental budget.

Perhaps your staff includes departments other than the law department. Mine included the Office of the Secretary, Records Management, Environmental Compliance, and the Ethics Office. Successfully leading those additional corporate units is a decathlon event all its own.

Ashton Eaton of the United States was one of the 28 decathletes at the 2016 Summer Olympics in Rio de Janeiro. Eaton competed in the 10 decathlon events. They included four races, 100 meters, 110 meter hurdles, 400 meters, and 1500 meters. The other six events were the long jump, high jump, shot put, discus throw, pole vault, and the javelin throw.

If you are not a diehard decathlon fan, what follows may surprise you. Eaton finished 1st in only two of the 10 events, the long jump and the 400 meter race. He finished 2nd in two other events. He was 3rd in one event. He finished 4th in another, 10th in another, 14th in another, and in his worst showing, the javelin throw, Eaton finished in 18th place.

He won the gold medal.

If you are ever tempted to ignore the advice in this chapter, and instead skip doing one or more of the tasks in your particular decathlon, consider this. The javelin throw was Ashton Eaton's worst decathlon skill. 18th place is nothing to brag about. In order to avoid appearing mediocre against the other contestants, he might have considered just skipping the event.

But by participating in the javelin throw, and getting the points awarded for 18th place, Eaton won the gold medal. If he had skipped the javelin throw, he would not have won gold. He would not even have been on the medal stand. His final standing in the competition would have been 12th place.

Whichever General Counsel decathlon event is the one in which you would finish 18th, just remember that you still have to show up for it and do it as well as you can. It may be the difference between your ultimate success or clearing out your desk to make room for its next occupant.

My boss' boss left Navistar in 1986, just after my fifth anniversary in the Law Department. I liked him. He was a good lawyer and a good manager. He had spent over a quarter of a century in the Law Department. He never became General Counsel. He ended his career as the Law Department's second in command.

On one of his last days at the Company, I took him out to lunch. We toasted his upcoming retirement. I reminded him about the time when we had a big layoff just after I started working for the Company and I thought I was going to be fired, and how he came to my office and told me that I wasn't. I thanked him for that. We talked some more. And then he said to me, "Covey, you should stick with this. One day you are going to be the General Counsel. I'll tell you why. Because you're smart. Not as smart as your current boss, but you're smart. And," he said with a grin, "you're a good bullshitter. Not as good as I am, but you're good."

In his mind, being named General Counsel required that you successfully compete in two events, intelligence and bullshitting. In his view, I wasn't in first place in either. In his view, I didn't need to be. It was enough that I would finish in second place in both events.

I don't think I got a lot smarter and I am almost certain that I didn't get any better at bullshitting. But eighteen years after that farewell lunch, his prediction came true.

I rest my case.

CHAPTER 26

Be the Person the CEO Wants In That Small Conference Room

Lots of scholarly articles have been written about who exactly is the General Counsel's client. The general consensus is that it is the corporation that employs him or her, which isn't a lot of help. We all learned in law school that a corporation is deemed to be a person. But it's not a person you can talk to. Who embodies the corporation? The Board of Directors? The shareholders? The executive officers?

Whatever opinion you have on the question, the fact is that on a day to day basis, your client is the CEO. The CEO is the person to whom you report, unless your corporation decides you should report to someone else, which, in my opinion, is a mistake. But I digress.

I worked with and for a half dozen CEOs. Each of them faced significant challenges and had to make tough decisions. It's the nature of the job. And for each of them, there was at least one crisis that was far tougher than the others, a crisis that made other crises look routine. I called it the CEO Moment.

Every CEO Moment was different but each one had several things in common. The crisis was unexpected. The consequences of any decision were huge. And the knowledge needed to decide what to do next was in one or more fields in which the CEO had no, or virtually no, prior experience.

One Navistar CEO had to deal with retiree health care costs. His CEO Moment required detailed knowledge of health care practices and trends, new accounting pronouncements, how to successfully deal with the UAW, class action lawsuit tactics, and the pros and cons of a corporate bankruptcy. He was not a lawyer. His familiarity with health care was minimal, as was his experience with the UAW, and although his background was in finance, he was not an accountant.

Another Navistar CEO faced his CEO Moment in the area of corporate governance. He had to learn about non-voting common stock, standstill agreements, ERISA diversification principles and secondary stock offerings. His background was in mechanical engineering.

If I were writing a book about CEOs, my suggestion for the Board of Directors would be that they consider only those candidates they believe can handle CEO Moments.

The CEO Moments I witnessed may have had different subject matters, but each CEO responded in the same way. They rapidly learned what they didn't know. They met with a small group of advisors to figure out what to do. The CFO. The General Counsel. Depending on the nature of the crisis, maybe one other person, maybe two. There are times when a town hall meeting is appropriate and times when the decision-making group has to fit into a small conference room.

I have been in that small conference room on more than one occasion. In every one of them, each of the participants contributed insights and advice that went beyond their core specialty. It is when you get to fulfill the dual role of "Attorney and Counselor at Law". At those times, you will be glad that you know so much about the business and the issues that extend beyond the Law Department.

During the time that I was General Counsel, a group of executives, including the CEO, met on a periodic basis to discuss succession candidates for the Company's top jobs. One of the positions discussed was the General Counsel position, my job. The last time we met to discuss who should be my successor before I began my retirement, this is what I said to the CEO.

"Lots of attorneys have the skills and intelligence to be the General Counsel. But it comes down to what I call the CEO Moment, that moment when you, the CEO, are faced with a gigantic problem and you have to figure out what to do next. It is ironic, but in my experience every CEO Moment involves one or more topics about which you, the CEO, know practically nothing. At those times, this is what you will do, what all of your predecessors have done. You will call a meeting. It will be held in a small conference room. The conference room will be small because you will only invite a few people. One or more subject matter experts may attend, depending on the type of crisis. But you always will invite your Chief Financial Officer. Because whatever you decide, it will have a cost, and you need your CFO to tell you what that cost will be. And you always will invite your General Counsel. Because CEO Moments always carry legal risks. So when all is said and done, the question you should ask yourself in deciding who should be the next General Counsel is this. What lawyer do I want to have with me in that small conference room?"

If you want to be the General Counsel, you need to be that lawyer.